IMAGINE

THE SIMPLE STEPS TO SUCCESS

DUSTIN MATTHEWS

Imagine
©2021, Dustin Matthews

ISBN: 978-1-09835-627-9
ISBN eBook: 978-1-09835-628-6

EDITOR'S NOTE

Intended to help readers find meaning and purpose in their lives, this self-help book serves as guide to discovering your "Self," letting go of negative energy and habits, and becoming the person you want to be. The author, a recovered addict, describes his journey to help readers find peace, happiness, and enlightenment, through the use of his "simple steps." Delving into details on every aspect of life that prevent people from finding their true potential, the book provides solutions and alternatives. With dedication, work, and understanding the "steps," it will become clear how everyone can achieve true spirituality, knowledge, and success. Inspiring quotes interspersed throughout the text are not only uplifting but build on the various messages. Complete with charts, exercises, and tools, readers will learn how to apply the messages (and "steps") to their own lives.

TABLE OF CONTENTS

INTRODUCTION

Hello, my name is Dustin Matthews, and I'm currently a professor at Maharishi International University in Fairfield, IA. I first began writing this book seven years ago when I was finishing a master's degree in education and coaching college football at Plymouth State University in Plymouth, NH, of the United States. I was 23 years old then and started writing this as a playbook for the running backs I was coaching, and called it *The Running Back Code*. But over time, it has developed into something more: *IMAGINE: The Simple Steps to Success.*

What had started out as a playbook with all my secrets for the football players I was coaching slowly transformed into a playbook for life. This book is a collected work of objective knowledge, personal (subjective) experience, spiritual wisdom, philosophical contemplation, and, what I consider, humorous self-talk to try and help others, whether you play football or not. The purpose of this book is to provide practical solutions to find meaning and purpose in your own lives and how to work progressively in the direction of your own dreams. It's important to understand my definition of success may vary from yours, and I will explain that as well. Please be patient and trust me when I say that reading this book and applying some of what I'll discuss will impact you in a positive and profound way. First, I'll share a little bit about what inspired me to write this book so you can grasp the bigger picture.

School was always rather easy and boring for me, and I got by without too much effort. I realized in college the more effort and energy that I put into something, the better I usually did. I always found myself desiring to learn more, but I wasn't challenged enough in the ways that I needed. I suppose that's my excuse for experimenting with drugs and alcohol as much as I did. I wasn't satisfied with my life as it was, so I started seeking something more.

To unpack all the social/mental conditioning and psychological trauma that led me to do the things I've done, I'd need a much longer book, so I'll keep it concise in this introduction to cut to the chase and get you the goods. I understand some might be like me and just want to read the table of contents to find what's currently most relevant to them and just read that. That's fine. However, if you bear with me through this "Introduction," you'll gain a better understanding of why I'm writing this book, and how following the steps I've laid out can help you make the changes that you want to be able to live a healthier, happier, more successful life. Believe it or not, there is a method to my madness.

As a college football player, I worked my hardest to try and fulfill my potential, but something inside was dissatisfied. In high school, I had been cheated on and felt betrayed by lovers and friends, and regardless of the injuries and obstacles I overcame to play college football, let alone become the captain and starting fullback as a senior and fifth year senior, there was something inside that felt empty. I was raging with self-defeat, depression, guilt, shame, and regret. These lingering feelings were some of the factors that led me to making some terrible decisions including when I almost overdosed on cocaine.

Who was I in my darkest hour? Captain of the football team with a GPA above 3.0. Women loved me. Friends loved me. Family loved me. On the surface, I had a great life. But in my darkest hour, I lay in bed from 3 to 9 a.m. fighting just to keep breathing. I'd spent another night drinking and doing cocaine. At that point, my depression and dissatisfaction with life was so deep, it felt like cocaine was the only thing that seemed to temporarily relieve the suffering. On the night that I almost overdosed, I'd snorted so much cocaine that both my nostrils were bleeding, but I continued to ingest more cocaine. I couldn't stop myself. I just wanted the pain to end.

That night, I realized that I was an addict and needed to change, or I was going to kill myself by overdosing on purpose or accidentally. I saw the simple truth of how precious life is and how we are always just a breath away from what lies beyond what we call life. As I lay in my bed without the strength to even cry, I wrote a note to my mother and father and sister. It took all my strength just to hold a pen and write, *I love you, Mom. I love you, Dad. I love you Emilia. I'm sorry.*

I lay in my bed, and in my thoughts, I pleaded for God to save me. I tried to bargain with God and said, "If you save me now, I'll do anything for you." I tried to sleep, but each time, I felt my body go into sleep mode, my breath started to leave my body and "I" went with it. I started to identify with my breath more than my body. Or, what I now call my, "Conscious Awareness." Every time my breath left my body, "I" went with it outside of my body and was formless and expanded. I forced myself to breathe life back into my body and stay "alive." From 3 to 9 a.m., I prayed to God and begged for my life, just trying to keep my breath in my body. I wasn't ready to die just yet.

What I realized from this experience was that there was something more to life and death. There was something beyond the human body and senses and intellectual comprehension, but the best word to try and define it would be *consciousness.* A more in-depth description would be the omnipresent eternal consciousness that encompasses all of existence. The soul or consciousness that experiences life within a body perceived through the mind and the senses.

Throughout my college years, I realized that my individual performance in the classroom and on the football field was affected by my mental state, which was affected by many factors including the use of drugs and alcohol. I experienced firsthand the effects of a lot of different drugs, those that would get me up and pumped for practice and games like caffeine (yes, it is a drug) as well as Adderall that is a form of amphetamine. I used other drugs and alcohol to alleviate mental, emotional, and physical pain after the games. Primarily, alcohol and cocaine. Cocaine was personally my worst addiction because it worked so quickly and temporarily alleviated physical pain and heavy emotional pain, like depression. But when the high ended and reality crept back in, it was a living hell.

I didn't use drugs every day during my playing career in college; in fact, I made the most progress when I was able to stay sober and clean, focusing on my performance as a student and athlete. Regardless of what people may think about my substance use, I always believed deep down that I was a good person and cared very much about the welfare of others. I didn't want to use drugs and alcohol, but those were the only things I knew of that alleviated my stress, pain, and suffering at the time.

I realize now there were many factors that led to me using drugs and alcohol. I was in a cycle that was hard to break out of and knew of no other means to reduce my stress. Physical and emotional pain and suffering were two main reasons for my drug and alcohol abuse as well as the pressure I felt to perform at a high level. I played through a separated AC joint twice in my playing career—once as a senior in high school, which put me out for two weeks, and once again in college, which put me out for two months. The reason I was a redshirt or fifth year senior in college was because I had hip surgery as a sophomore in college and was told never to play football again. My response to the doctor was two popular words that I don't think should be used in this book. They started with *F* and ended with *U*.

There were times I felt guilty and ashamed wishing I was a better person who made better decisions that would be accepted by the people I looked up to, including my parents, my coaches, my teammates, my professors, my Self, and God. I wished I'd made it and could have played at a higher level and didn't abuse drugs and alcohol, but I did what I did, and I've learned from it. It wasn't until I was clean and sober that all of this realization and understanding became clear. Self-realization smacked me in the face at first, but I learned to accept and forgive myself for my past and know that others can do the same for themselves.

When I started this book, I thought I'd realized all of my "wrongs" and "rights" and could discern between good and bad decisions. I wanted to write a book for the younger guys I was coaching, so they wouldn't make the same mistakes that I had. I learned the *hard way* and wanted to make it easier for players who still had a chance to develop and fulfill their potential. For me, as a college athlete, the ship had sailed.

Self-Possessed

When I first got sober, I was coaching and one night during preseason football camp I was the last one in the office. I began writing this playbook when a strange sense of awareness came over me, and it felt like something was writing through me. It was unlike anything I had ever felt before, and I became intensely curious about this new state of mind. It was an experience that I've explored for the past seven years and have now come to understand as "being in the flow" or experiencing a "higher state of consciousness."

I was captivated by the feeling and couldn't stop writing. It's been seven years since I began writing this book, but I've never stopped writing it. Just like "life" and the "mind," this book has been a process of adapting and integrating knowledge and experience. This book is a combination of practicality and spirituality that includes the most important things that have impacted my life, my mind, and my growth.

The feeling of effortlessness and peace that came over me when I wrote was like being possessed by "God." It was as if thoughts were delivered into my mind from an elevated source beyond what I'd consider myself able to comprehend. It was as if I had access to all knowledge by just the smallest intention of a thought, which was then answered by another thought. It was a continuous stream of consciousness flowing through me and I was there allowing "It" to write through me.

Although "It" was a mystery to me at the time, I believe this was a discovery of my own intuition or connection with the Divine/God. I was acutely aware of my surroundings and not just my own thoughts and feelings but the thoughts and feelings of others. I didn't grow up in a strictly religious or very spiritual family, so these types of things weren't really talked about. I went to Sunday School, but after that, I pretty much discovered things on my own.

About a year after the onset of this newfound awareness, I went to Maharishi International University and earned a master's degree in Vedic Science, which is the science and technology of consciousness. In Vedic terms, the experience I encountered when I started this book was called "Ritambhara Prajna," which means, the "truth bearing intellect" or as Lord

Krishna explains it, "Righteous Knowledge." This phenomenon has also been explained in the Hermetic Principles as the "All Mind." In Christianity, it is often described with words like the "Holy Spirit" or "God," in Buddhism—"Thy Self," in *The Urantia Book*—"The God Fragment," and as Maharishi Mahesh Yogi calls it "Pure Consciousness" or "The Absolute." (Mahesh Yogi, 1963)

I didn't know it at the time and although it was new to me, this "Self" discovery has been explored by many people throughout history. This "Self" discovery or "God" realization opened me to a stronger connection and possession, in the best way possible. An unquenchable thirst for knowledge continues as I try to understand this infinitely beautiful phenomenon. It's interesting to me trying to explain this because "It is Everything, and Nothing." The Unified Field. Pure Consciousness. God. And we're All a part of That.

You might be thinking, "What the hell is this guy talking about?" "Why is he capitalizing so many words?" You might be completely engaged and absorbing this knowledge as you may have experienced something similar within you and just needed to be reminded. I'm talking about the part of every human that deep, down inside, "Knows" or "feels like they know." It might still be uncertain or unclear, but you want to trust it. But doubt and skepticism may be turning your wheels and clouding your mind. It's okay; I've been there. Just keep breathing.

The part of you that "Knows" is your individual connection to the "All Mind" or "Pure Consciousness" or "God" or "Spirit" or "Higher Self." These are all tag words, which are trying to explain the same thing. And that pouty little doubter inside is your "ego," your "small mind" or "small self," and the fear and skepticism is the part of you that divides and thinks, "no, no, no, me, me, me."

But that part of you is insignificant in comparison to your "Higher Self." Access is free and always available from anywhere at any time. There is no password for the Wi-Fi to the Universe. Everyone is connected; it is just a matter of how refined your perception is to receive information and comprehend it. God is infinite. Man was created in the image of God. You are infinite. Let's get rid of those limiting beliefs so you can start to see for your Self.

One of the reasons I'm so interested in spirituality/God/consciousness/ truth/knowledge is because I feel that my purpose is to teach people how to live happier and healthier lives. I've experienced negative emotions and sought truth and knowledge for many years and hope to help those who are experiencing negativity move through and away from it. Or for those who need a little pick-me-up, I hope to inspire you to get out of your own way and move in the direction you want with your life.

My goal is to point you in the direction of self-reflection or subjective knowledge. I hope to bridge the communication gap between the many different fields of knowledge and connect and show the commonalities between the various theories and concepts. This book is an attempt to see the unity in new-age science and world religion. Words. Words. Words.

What are words but labels we've created to help us classify, define, understand, and conceptualize things? What are sentences but coherently organized thoughts and words? But in what language are those thoughts and sentences? How many different languages are there? Is there a universal language? What about emotion, feeling, and energy? How can we transcend the limitations of language, words, thoughts, emotions, feelings, and energy? Why do we need to go beyond objective means? Because there is more to life than meets the eye. Everything is Subjective. You are the subject. Consciousness is the universal experience.

How do you access this "consciousness?" You already are. You picked up this book for a reason. You're curious. You seek knowledge. It's just a matter of how finely in tuned you are. How "Consciously Aware" you are of your "Self." Do you identify with your body or your "consciousness?" You have the ability to access all the answers you seek, within you. My goal is to help get you started.

An analogy to explain it, think of a static-y radio station. The amount of static going through your mind or body is how stress, anxiety, fear, doubt, and negativity are jamming your signals. An old radio with tons of dust needs to be tuned up. How do you refine or tune up your radio (mind and body)? Sleep, meditation, physical activity, and proper nutrition are a few great things to start with, but we'll get to that later.

Returning to when I first started feeling a connection to the mysterious world within, it stuck with me and I wanted to learn more about it. At the end of that football season and spending hours writing this book, I realized if I wanted to pursue something other than playing and coaching football meant making a decision to make a change. No more waiting. I felt a higher calling and had the faith to follow my intuition regardless of the unknowns.

It was very hard walking away from football because it was all I'd ever wanted growing up and all I knew and loved. However, having glimpsed the "flow state" or "higher state of consciousness," I became possessed with seeking more knowledge. I moved back into my parents' house and learned the practice of Transcendental Meditation. Within six months, I was on my way to Maharishi International University in Fairfield, IA to get a second master's degree in Maharishi's Vedic Science. Vedic science comes from the word "Veda" meaning "Knowledge," so I like to call it the science of knowledge.

One of the things we learned was the relationship between the knower, the process of knowing and the known. In other words, Rishi (Knower), Devata (Process of Knowing), and Chandas (Known). So, we have you (the Knower), reading (the Process of Knowing) this book (the Known). Sounds simple right? But this threefold process of gaining knowledge is much more complex than just reading.

For instance, you are probably reading this and relating it to other things you've read that seem familiar, you're integrating what you're reading with your previous knowledge/experience/beliefs and the neurons in your brain are firing around making connections. The process includes taking in information and integrating it with what you already have in your own cup. You, the subject or Knower are the cup that has the capacity to gain knowledge. But what's in your cup already? Does your cup have a lid on it? Is there a hole in your cup? Looking within is the start to identifying what's in your cup and how to start expanding the size of your cup. Because let's be honest, who doesn't want a bigger cup?

The Known. What is it you're taking in? Gaining objective knowledge can be like panning for gold. You have to filter out the rough stuff and look for that shining glimmer of truth. If you're in tune with your Self, you'll be able to identify/discern the truth from the gibberish. It's like tuning an instrument, if it's in tune it'll feel right and resonate with you. If it's off, you'll feel that too.

Anyways, for those interested in accolades and credentials, I currently have three degrees: a bachelor's degree in Physical Education from Plymouth State University, a master's degree in Education from Plymouth State University, and a master's degree in Maharishi's Vedic Science from Maharishi International University. However, of all this knowledge, the simple practice of Transcendental Meditation continues to be the most beneficial and fulfilling thing I've learned. Simply put, if you only take one thing from this book, I hope it will be learning the practice of Transcendental Meditation.

How to Best Use This Book

In this book, I do my best to explain the reasoning behind the steps but understand I'm summarizing and simplifying the steps so you can begin applying them right away without fumbling around in the dark hoping something will work for you. This is what worked for me. So, I know with a little effort it can work for anyone. As you will discover, everything is a matter of focused attention and energy.

If you wish to gain a better understanding or more in-depth knowledge of something specific, I suggest also conducting your own personal research. I've learned that trying something is one of the best ways to learn, so go and experience things for yourself. Please. Experience is the best teacher. Life teaches the greatest lessons. You'll learn more by applying the knowledge in this book than just reading it.

If you're anything like me, you can be stubborn or have a hard time believing something just because someone says it. A healthy amount of doubt or skepticism is acceptable for those seeking "truth." But when you have a "subjective experience," you learn on a whole new level. There is only so much we can learn without truly experiencing it, so please trust yourselves to let go and see what happens. You may like what you discover.

This is not permission to do something you know is wrong. Karma in Vedic terminology means action and actions have consequences. But I will discuss karma/action/cause and effect later. For now, continue reading the book in the order I put it to gain a good basis of understanding or foundation of knowledge to start living a better life.

Life is a process of self-discovery, and the word "enlightenment" is often thrown around like it's the end goal for a human being becoming a spiritual being. However, we are already spiritual beings and evolution is just the process of remembering and enlivening that. Sometimes, "enlightening" experiences happen, like a flash of clarity, but for the most part, it's not always going to be like a light switch that flips from off to on; it's like a dimmer switch that is gradually turned up over time through life, knowledge, and experience.

In the beginning of my search for meaning I read a lot of *self-help books* and *religious* or *spiritual texts*. I began to realize that the majority of what I'd been reading was sprinkled with "Truth" or "Right Knowledge" from the "All Mind," "Pure Consciousness," "God," or the "Universe." These are just labels or tag words used throughout the ages in an effort to explain the layers of reality in existence so people in different times and cultures could understand or try to make sense/peace with themselves and others. The "Aha" moment is a "revelation" or "eureka," an "enlightening thought" or a glimpse of "Pure Consciousness" when your brain finally makes a connection between concepts and understands reality at a deeper level. Can you see that all the different words, concepts, language styles, and religions are trying to explain the same thing or essence of "Absolute Reality," the "Unified Field," the "All Mind" or "God?" *It's All within You.*

If you are experiencing confusion, pain, suffering, doubt, fear, worry, sadness, addiction, depression, anxiety, and so on, I hope to lead you through the steps you can take to overcome these. If you are searching for the "Right Knowledge," my goal is to remind you that the "Right Knowledge" is already within you. All you have to do is start taking the steps I've laid out for you to have access to the source of knowledge within at all times.

Accepting that this book is a process of learning and lifestyle adaptation is essential. A complete transformation may not happen overnight; it will take effort and attention, practice, patience, and commitment. I hope you understand you can become a better person and live a happier, healthier, more fulfilling life. But you have to really want to change and be willing to apply the knowledge in this book. It won't just happen for you. I can recommend what steps to take but you'll need to choose to walk them on your own.

I know that beginning the process of self-knowledge and self-discovery can be difficult. So, relax. Try to breathe deeply as you continue reading. Start from where you are. You don't have to commit your life to this if you don't want to. Just start with one day at a time—one step at a time. Take what you feel you need at the time. Anytime you feel flustered or an intense emotion overtakes you, take a deep breath, in through the nose and out through the mouth. You're right where you belong. Then continue.

What you put your attention on grows stronger in your life.

-MAHARISHI MAHESH YOGI

STEP 1:
DEVELOP THE RIGHT MINDSET

The first step is to develop the right mindset. In order to accomplish this, I will discuss some of the ways it can be done. Being open to receiving new knowledge is the most important thing to consider. So, keep an open mind. Remember, you are the cup (the Knower). Keep the lid open so you can gain more knowledge.

Perspective

The main thing I wish to convey is that everything is a matter of "perspective." The idea of the person you hope to become is just that, an idea. What will live on longer—your human body or the immortal spirit and consciousness within you?

Ripples, waves, drops in the ocean. Recognize you are but a drop in an ocean. Recognize you are the ocean in a drop. Thy Self in the Universe. The Universe in thy Self.

Do we recognize our universality? Do we *see* the similarities we all have with one another? Human beings on planet Earth. We all have the same size eyes. Do we all desire love, truth, knowledge, happiness? Do we cling to our perspective in order to have stability or a sense of control within our ever-changing environment? Do we recognize the limitations within our own thoughts? Are we consciously able to perceive that which we desire? Are we able to perceive consciousness or is consciousness the perceiver?

Does the philosophical perspective to life make you wonder if individual beliefs have an effect on the ability to manifest things into the environment? Are you able to identify your beliefs? Are you conscious of your beliefs or do you have some beliefs that may be unconscious based on what you've been taught to believe? Can you see how our beliefs have guided us through our lives whether consciously or unconsciously?

Basically, I'm a *self-proclaimed genius* who has finally figured my Self out after years of depression, drug and alcohol abuse, and therapy couldn't. Is this Narcissism? I don't know. Sometimes I laugh at my Self for all of the different perspectives I've held at one time or another. Letting go of them can be hard at first. But humans shed their egos like snakes shed their skins. Let it go. Let it grow.

I wanted to be a professional football player, but I only made it to Division III. I've had hip surgery, separated both shoulders, and probably suffered a little brain damage. I didn't make it to the NFL; life goes on. I've recorded a few rap albums, written this self-help book, and realized God. I wish I'd figured out this thing we call "reality" at a younger age. But now my goal is to help you recognize your limitless potential so you can live the life of your dreams.

Right View and the Golden Rule

Our views or perspectives are an accumulation of social and mental conditioning. Our view, perspective, or understanding of life is a symptom of conditioning, rather than a pure observation of potential choices. According to early Buddhist texts, Buddha, having attained the state of "enlightenment" or the "unconditioned mind," is said to have "passed beyond the bondage, tie, greed, obsession, acceptance, attachment, and lust of view."

In Buddhism, it has been said that those who wish to experience nirvana must free themselves from everything binding them to the world, including philosophical and religious doctrines. "Right view" is the first part of the Noble Eightfold Path, which ultimately leads not to holding the correct views, but to a detached form of cognition, *nirvana*. Nirvana is a term used for the state of enlightenment that can be reached through the practice of meditation. But this state of enlightenment has also been referred to as *Samadhi*. In my experience, the term *Nirvana* is used more often in Buddhism, while *Samadhi* is used more often in Hinduism or the Vedic Tradition. But the attainment of either is said to come from some form of meditation practice.

In Buddhism, the term *right view* or *right understanding* is basically about having the correct attitude toward life. This is explained by the system of karma and the cycle of rebirth. It states that our actions have consequences, that death is not the end, and our actions and beliefs also have consequences after death, and that Buddha followed and taught a successful path to liberation or freedom from suffering.

This sounds similar to Christianity. But in Christianity, Jesus said, *I am the way, and the truth, and the life. No one comes to the Father except through me* (John 14:6). How can I say this so you understand? Jesus and Buddha were both enlightened beings. They were both God-realized or Self-realized and tried to teach people of their times how to accept God into their lives.

The way I see it is that God is Within Everything. I think God can be realized/perceived/experienced/manifested/cultivated within by human beings through our own evolution of consciousness. I believe different people past and present have accepted God and allowed God to work through them. There will always be a choice. So for me, I choose to surrender through prayer, meditation, and contemplation and try to learn to be a channel for the Divine to use. I love Jesus, Buddha, Krishna, and all the enlightened masters.

To protect the righteous and destroy the wicked, to establish dharma firmly, I take birth age after age.

-LORD KRISHNA, BHAGAVAD GITA, CH. 4 V. 8

I know religion can be a controversial subject for some, but in my life, I've tried to see the good in all religions. I believe religions are like rivers, all coming from the same source. And I believe God to be the source of All. I've studied a few different religions and I'm not afraid to try and see from different perspectives. I still remember the "Golden Rule," which was created because it is the one thing almost all cultures and religions have in common.

Treat others the way you want to be treated.

-THE GOLDEN RULE

One should never do something to others that one would regard as an injury to one's own self. In brief, this is Dharma. Anything else is succumbing to desire.

-MAHĀBHĀRATA

If the entire Dharma can be said in a few words, then it is—that which is unfavorable to us, do not do that to others.

-PADMA PURANA

One who, while himself seeking happiness, oppresses with violence other beings who also desire happiness, will not attain happiness hereafter.

-DHAMMAPADA

Hurt not others in ways that you yourself would find hurtful.

-UDANAVARGA

Do not do to others that which angers you when they do it to you.

-ISOCRATES

Treat your inferior as you would wish your superior to treat you.

-SENECA THE YOUNGER

You shall not take vengeance or bear a grudge against your kinsfolk. Love your neighbor as yourself: I am the LORD.

-LEVITICUS

Love your fellow as yourself.

-RABBI AKIVA

What is hateful to you, do not do to your fellow: this is the whole Torah; the rest is the explanation; go and learn.

-SHABBAT

For all the law is fulfilled in one word, even in this; Thou shalt love thy neighbor as thyself.

-GALATIANS

None of you [truly] believes until he wishes for his brother what he wishes for himself.

-AN-NAWAWI'S 40 HADITH

In happiness and suffering, in joy and grief, we should regard all creatures as we regard our own self.

-LORD MAHAVIRA

Precious like jewels are the minds of all. To hurt them is not at all good. If thou desirest thy Beloved, then hurt thou not anyone's heart.

-GURU ARJAN DEV JI

What you do not want done to yourself, do not do to others.

-CONFUCIUS

The sage has no interest of his own, but takes the interests of the people as his own. He is kind to the kind; he is also kind to the unkind: for Virtue is kind. He is faithful to the faithful; he is also faithful to the unfaithful: for Virtue is faithful.

-TAO TE CHING

Try to treat others as you would want them to treat you.

-L. RON HUBBARD

One who is going to take a pointed stick to pinch a baby bird should first try it on himself to feel how it hurts.

-YORUBA PROVER

Do not do to others what you would not want them to do to you. [is] (…) the single greatest, simplest, and most important moral axiom humanity has ever invented, one which reappears in the writings of almost every culture and religion throughout history, the one we know as the Golden Rule. Moral directives do not need to be complex or obscure to be worthwhile, and in fact, it is precisely this rule's simplicity which makes it great. It is easy to come up with, easy to understand,

and easy to apply, and these three things are the hallmarks of a strong and healthy moral system. The idea behind it is readily graspable: before performing an action which might harm another person, try to imagine yourself in their position, and consider whether you would want to be the recipient of that action. If you would not want to be in such a position, the other person probably would not either, and so you should not do it. It is the basic and fundamental human trait of empathy, the ability to vicariously experience how another is feeling, that makes this possible, and it is the principle of empathy by which we should live our lives.

-ADAM LEE

Truth is one, but the wise know it as many; God is one, but we can approach Him in many ways.

-THE RIG VEDA

What I've learned from studying different religions is that God doesn't discriminate. God loves all of us. When I was an elementary school physical education teacher, the kids always loved playing dodgeball. I'd divide the kids into teams as evenly and equally as possible. I didn't care which side won as long as it was fair, and they all had fun.

During the dodgeball games, if I saw someone get hit and lie about it, then I had to intervene and be the judge, and say, "Hey you got hit; go to jail." I also kept an eye on which team was winning. As I watched the game progress if one team was taking a beating, I would help the underdog team to even out the playing field. I would kick loose balls to their side, so they had "more ammo," and sometimes I'd even jump in and join the losing team. When I joined the losing team, both teams would get all excited and usually I would aim to take out the opposing team's best players just to show them "who was boss."

Although, this analogy is a bit of a joke. I think God can and does work in the Universe in anyway possible. God wants everyone to get along and be happy and have fun and tries to let us, his children, work things out on our own. But when it gets to the point where the children lose their way, God works in mysterious ways and can intervene. Sometimes as a gym teacher playing dodgeball. Righteousness will be restored.

Do you have the patience to wait until your mud settles and the water is clear?

-LAO TZU, TAO TE CHING

For everyone who exalts himself will be humbled, and everyone who humbles himself will be exalted.

-JESUS CHRIST

So, what's the point I'm trying to make? Don't let the evil divide. Look for the good in others. See beyond gender, color, and creed. Fear not. Breathe. My purpose is not to have anyone conform to a certain religion. I'm only reminding you to seek the "Truth" within. Religious scriptures to the seers of "Truth" are like wells in an oasis with fresh water all around. When you realize God, you realize all paths, no matter how different, eventually lead to the same destination and stem from the same source. The speed of an individual's evolution is more dependent on the purity and will of that person's soul to know the "Truth" than the religious doctrines and cultural customs they were born into.

This is an important thing to consider because no matter what you want in life, what you give is what you will get. I might come across as preachy but there is a reason that spiritual knowledge is one of the main focuses of this book. Because I have found it to be the most important. Yes, I still have other desires in the material world, and you can too. But understanding how things work will help you navigate your way through life a bit easier. So, take it easy. Try not to be too quick to label and judge things or people.

Also, keep in mind that I'm trying to help you accelerate your learning and growth. It took me years of living, studying, and meditating to develop my mindset, skills, and lifestyle. Now, I would like to share what is most important in a precise and concise way. There are enough gems in this book to last you a lifetime. But you'll have to be the one to apply the knowledge.

Growing Up versus Taking Responsibility

"It's time to grow up." Anyone ever hear that before? What does it really mean?

Biologically, we all grow up at the same rate. Time will do that for us. But the context in which I've heard this phrase during my life was most often from someone's perspective, usually older, who thought I needed to act more maturely or take responsibility or be more realistic (by thinking or being more like them).

I was told to grow up many times in my life, but I was never told how. What does it really mean to "grow up?" To take responsibility? To be financially independent?

Taking responsibility is a choice and it can be difficult to take responsibility for yourself and your actions. In order to really take responsibility, there has to be a conscious choice. It is a process of maturity. And it is a necessity if you want to grow.

Think of someone immature. What does immaturity look like? Doing things and not accepting responsibility? Not thinking about the consequences of their actions? No doubt we've all been there at some time or another.

In order to mature, we need to learn. We can learn from others' mistakes. Sometimes, we learn from making mistakes, believe me I know, I've made a few. But immaturity is overcome by taking responsibility.

What does it mean to be unrealistic? To dream without a plan? To dream without taking action? What does it mean to be realistic? To plan and take action in the direction of your dream?

What I've learned from my mistakes has been to take responsibility, and I hope to teach what I've learned so others can learn what I wish I'd been taught at a younger age.

Accepting that you need to take responsibility for yourself and your actions will serve you well in the long run. However, you are the one that is responsible for applying the knowledge provided to help make the necessary changes you want to make in your life. You are the only one who can decide how you use it. The knowledge in this book will only work for you as much as you work for you. It worked and continues to work for me. So, I know with some effort, it can work for anyone, if they apply themselves.

Receptivity

Receptivity represents the willingness or openness to take in new information and new ideas. I like to think of receptivity like a sponge. Are you able to absorb information and new ideas?

Note: It is important to remember that being receptive to new information and new ideas does not mean you have to conform, adopt, or believe them to be true. It simply means you can take it in and process it. Working with new information is like blending your existing knowledge, past experiences, and memories with your newfound knowledge. This process of purification allows us to refine our perspective and integrate what we've learned.

The three-part process of knowledge consists of

- *Receptivity (absorption)*

- *Process (purification)*

- *Application (integration)*

What can I do to increase my receptivity?

- Sobriety brings clarity

- Adequate amount of quality sleep *(ideally 7 to 9 hours a night)*

- Meditation

- Listening nonjudgmentally

What things can hinder someone's receptivity?
- Fear/judgment

- Hate/bias

- Inadequate sleep

How can I increase the receptivity of others?
- Kindness/compassion/genuine care

- Honesty/truth/relativity

- Humor/stories/personal experience

The Planes of Existence

The Physical Plane

On the grossest level of existence is the physical plane, the Earthly plane or material plane. It is the grossest level of creation because of the accumulation or density of material or energy. This plane is our physical bodies and how we operate in a material world that appears in a limited perspective through our human senses. The search for objective knowledge in this plane comes from science and observation. What can we prove or know objectively? However, if our device (human physiology) is limited in its ability to perceive then the objective knowledge we gain will only take us so far. This is where the other planes of existence reveal themselves and their importance if we aim to evolve.

The Mental Plane

The mental plane is the plane of the mind, and includes thought, philosophy, contemplation, and meditation. This is the processing plane where we purify and integrate the wisdom or insight we receive from the spiritual plane with the knowledge and experience from the physical plane. This is where we process our experience and commune back and forth with the spiritual plane and the physical plane. Enlightening thoughts, good ideas, visions, cognitions, revelations, and divine inspiration are some examples we can experience while engaging faculties of the mental plane.

The Spiritual Plane

The spiritual plane of existence is the plane of existence that predominates within all other planes. No other plane can exist without the existence of the spiritual plane. The Infinite. The Absolute. The Unified Field. God. The Source of All Creation. The Great Spirit. The Force. The vast nothingness from which everything manifests. The Field of All Knowledge. Pure Consciousness. The Tao. Whatever you want to call *It*. It Is. Even without name or form. It still *Is*.

We have the ability to access the source of all creation within ourselves through the techniques mentioned in the mental plane. Meditation is the primary agent for increasing an individual's receptivity to connect with the Divine. The individual that cultivates their mind through meditation, prayer, contemplation, and surrender, can be inspired to act as a conduit accessing knowledge from the spiritual plane and delivering it through the mental plane to the physical plane. Through their work, they integrate Spirit into form. Think about the Messiah. Messiah means messenger. We All have the capacity to Know God.

The Process

So, you're open to receiving new information and new ideas. Good. Now let's start to understand how we process information and ideas. Like we touched upon briefly before as you're reading, you are actively engaged in the process of taking in new information and you may experience your own stimulating thoughts. This is part of the process of purification.

Memories from past experiences may surface and want to express themselves. You might experience flashes of thoughts that connect to something else you've read or heard. These brain connections are happening all the time. The term "Eureka" is used when a connection is made that feels like a profound discovery.

This process of how the mind works with new information is an ongoing process of taking in new information or stimulus and relating it to previous knowledge and experience. However, our previous experiences can have a predominating effect on our outlook if there were events that we were unable to process or understand.

Processing new information/experience with past knowledge/experience is like putting a puzzle together. From our past knowledge/experience we have an idea of what our puzzle looks like. The new information/experiences we have continue to add new pieces to the puzzle and can reveal new images or puzzle pieces we hadn't seen before. This requires us to work with our newfound perspective if we wish to have a clearer understanding of what the puzzle is going to look like.

We could let the pieces pile up and not tend to our puzzle but over time they will clutter our minds and lives to a point that we can no longer ignore. And I don't know about you, but a 1000-piece puzzle can seem overwhelming, so it's important to employ a few techniques to help you process and continue putting your puzzle together a little bit at a time.

So how can we become more efficient in our ability to process?

- *Sobriety, quality sleep, meditation, physical exercise, and proper nutrition*

The Work and the Wisdom

The work comes before the wisdom. The work is what initiates the process of gaining wisdom. The work is the tilling of the field. This field needs to be tilled for the crops to grow. The fruits of your labor will not just be the crops you've grown but the wisdom you gain from the work that you do.

Work in this sense doesn't just refer to work on the gross level of creation. There is work to be done on other planes of human existence. A balanced workload allows for the most natural flow of work and wisdom. We only need to till the field and plant the seeds. The seeds will grow on their own in their own time. As long as we have adequately prepared and set the proper conditions we just need to act and rest. The fruits of your labor will not come any faster from increasing the amount of anxiety or mental worry. We just need to water the seeds that we want to see grow.

Put in the work. Then rest. Put in the work. Then rest. Put in the work. Then rest.

The fruits will come naturally of their own accord, along with the wisdom. But work is our duty. We must continue to put in the work to continue to gain the fruits of our labor. The wisdom is what we gain from that process.

Two words come to mind in relation to work and wisdom, these are preparation and inspiration. *Preparation* means we've put in the work and made ourselves ready. We've developed our skills and become efficient enough to complete our duties and be of use. Preparation means we continuously set ourselves and our environment/conditions for success. We make the proper decisions and plan accordingly and have the ability to adapt to any changes that arise. But even this level of preparation comes from the wisdom of experience, the wisdom of doing the work.

Inspiration is the spark or influence that stimulates something within us to become extremely efficient and act in a powerful way. In order to act most efficiently when inspiration strikes we need to put in the work every day. We cannot just wait for inspiration and then decide to put in the work, by then it's too late. We must prepare ourselves by putting in the work every day. So that when inspiration does strike, we will be ready and able to act most efficiently. If we could ask Leonardo DaVinci if he was inspired the whole time he was painting "The Mona Lisa" or "The Last Supper" or was it a few moments of inspiration and many moments of diligent and disciplined work.

What about the years of work he put in before his most famous paintings? We all start somewhere. So, start putting in the work.

Keeping the Channel Open

To build off preparation and inspiration, it is important to implement a consistent and balanced routine. The fundamentals are safety, oxygen, water, food, and sleep. Make sure you are in a safe environment. Breathe deeply. Do what you need to do to make sure you have water to drink and food to eat. And get enough sleep. This does not mean you should kill or steal. But ensure that your basic human needs are met.

Maslow's Hierarchy of Needs states that there is a hierarchy of human needs that we need to meet in a sequential order to progress, evolve, or maximize our human potential (Maslow, 1943). By opening ourselves up to a higher power through the process of meditation, prayer, and surrender, we allow the conditions in our minds to receive guidance from within. This inner guidance system will lead us to the experiences or knowledge we need to grow. If it is a job we need, we will be presented with opportunities to work. If it is a relationship we need, we will be presented with opportunities to be in relationships. If it is solitude we need, we will be presented with that.

The idea here is to keep the channel open to receive the inspiration of spirit. The planes of existence we, as humans, are involved in consist of the human body, mind, and spirit. So, we have the physical, mental, and spiritual planes. Keeping the channel open means living in harmony with nature and coexisting and integrating what we learn from these different planes of existence.

So how do we keep the channel open?

- *Sobriety brings clarity*

- *Adequate amount of quality sleep (ideally 7 to 9 hours a night)*

- *Meditation*

- *Physical activity*

- *Proper nutrition*

- *Creative outlets (meaningful activity)*

Transcendental Meditation

In order to apply Step 1 and keep an open mind, as I have said and will continue to repeat, I think everyone should learn the practice of Transcendental Meditation. Of all the knowledge I've accumulated in my life, I value this practice with sincere devotion. Transcendental Meditation continues to provide me with peace of mind, thereby increasing my overall level of happiness and success in my life. Without this simple practice, I'm not sure I'd still be alive or writing this book. But I'm very grateful to still be here.

What Transcendental Meditation Has Done for Me

I learned Transcendental Meditation in December 2014 with my mother. Prior to learning Transcendental Meditation, I experienced a "higher state of consciousness" about six weeks before the experience when I first began writing this book as a football coach, which I mentioned in the introduction. I was 23 years old, depressed and hungover at my parents' house. I knew I had a drinking and drug problem and was depressed about where I was in life mentally, emotionally, career wise, and financially. It was about a year after I'd almost overdosed and prayed for God to save me, but my search continued.

I prayed to God and pleaded wholeheartedly for a clear sign as to what I needed to do with my life and somehow it was answered. That day, my cousin who lived in Boston and her half-sister Lucia who was from Spain visited my parents' house in Maine. After this meeting with Lucia, whose name means *the Light*, I started the process of consciously changing my life and writing this book.

When I first saw her, I experienced the present moment with a beauty, clarity, peace, and wonder I'd never encountered before. I was captivated by her eyes, her presence, and an amazing depth of silence. No depression, no worries, no fear, almost no thought, just pure presence. Although there was a language barrier between us, it felt as if we knew what the other was thinking and feeling. It was one of if not the most pure and beautiful human interactions I've had to date.

After meeting her, I quit drinking and doing drugs. I learned the practice of Transcendental Meditation and started writing a lot of poems and songs and books, including this one. I was enlivened with a new sense of energy I'd never experienced before. Love? I had finally seen *the Light*. Seriously? Yeah. The Lord works in mysterious ways. I guess God knew the best way to get my attention was in the form of the most beautiful woman ever. So, to my Light, thank you. I'm eternally grateful for your presence in my life.

Over time, I found the courage to reach out to her and we started emailing and talking more. And with sobriety, I had more clarity to create the life I imagined for my Self. I decided I wanted to pursue a career in music or writing or acting, so I quit coaching football and moved home to my parents' house, where I was working on music and doing some personal training on the side.

That's when I experienced an orb of white light about two feet in diameter on my closet door one night. I was asleep and woke up and saw a round white sphere of white light hovering in front of my closet door. At first, I thought it must be the moon shining in and reflecting off the river. So, I turned and looked toward the window, but the blinds were shut. When I turned back around to the closet door with the white orb, it was still there.

I reached for my phone on the nightstand thinking it might be the source of the light. My phone was not emitting any light. I stared at the white orb for a few minutes without fear or worry. It felt friendly and peaceful and mysterious. After another minute, it just dissipated. It was amazing. It appeared again a week later on the wall right in front of my bed. At the time, I didn't know what it was, but now looking back, I believe it was a spirit guide that had come to lead me.

About a month later, I ended up going to Maharishi International University, where I studied Vedic Science. I learned the Transcendental Meditation Siddhi Program, which is an addition to the practice of Transcendental Meditation. I transformed what started out as a football playbook called

The Running Back Code into *IMAGINE: The Simple Steps to Success.* I've also recorded over 100 songs and released a few separate music albums.

My devotion to my Self and my own growth allowed me to make the changes I wanted to make in my life. It has provided me with inner peace and clarity. It has helped me connect the dots from my past that have all led me to where I am now. From connecting these dots, I was able to see how these experiences were guiding and molding me to become the person I wanted to become.

Why I Think Transcendental Meditation Is So Important: Isn't It Hard Work and Dedication That Got Me to Do These Things?

Transcendental Meditation is like the fuel that keeps me going. I think of it as spiritual energy that allows me to do whatever I put my mind to. It is how I experience a deeper connection with God/My Self/The Universe. Without it, I'd probably still be drinking and doing drugs to relieve my stress, anxiety, and depression. Instead, I meditate. I look within. It's an alternative practice to relieve stress, but it's also much more than that.

Yes, it takes effort and dedication to achieve goals, but it is also important to work smarter, not just harder. Scientific studies on Transcendental Meditation support its positive effects on cognition, increased IQ, increased emotional intelligence, alleviation of anxiety, depression, and stress, boosting self-confidence, improving reaction speed, lowering risk for heart disease, lowering blood pressure, improving sleep, and more. So, there are loads of benefits for all types of people.

The brain waves produced during the practice of Transcendental Meditation are called Alpha 1 brainwaves, which are assimilated to super learning and a more coherent style of brain functioning. There have been loads of studies done to validate the benefits of practicing Transcendental Meditation for anyone who doubts its effects. But my advice is just to try it for yourself.

Why Is *Transcendental Meditation* the Secret Step to Take to Success?

First, my personal definition of success might differ from yours. I think success is a feeling of accomplishment or fulfillment that can also be related to happiness. I think if success is to be measured objectively it would need to be goal oriented. If I am happy, am I successful? If that is my goal, how will we measure it? If my goal is to make a certain salary, then my success will depend on if I've reached the desired salary.

Transcendental Meditation is the *secret step* to take because it allows each individual to access a place within themselves and identify what it is they truly want and how they can manifest that into their reality. It allowed me to first identify my own personal definition of success and aligned my thinking to prioritize my life vision around objective goals and then take the appropriate steps to achieve them. These goals will vary from person to person, but the fuel for my success in doing what is necessary to achieve my long-term goals comes from the consistent practice of Transcendental Meditation.

The mind is a powerful tool. If we focus our attention or awareness on refining our minds, we can improve the functioning of our mind and harness the power of our awareness which gives us the ability to direct our energy in whatever way we choose. With that, we can recognize all possibilities. However, purity of heart also plays a role in the refinement of the mind. More on that later.

Is *Transcendental Meditation* a Science or Religion?

When it comes to science and religion, I believe they are two sides of the same coin. I use language from both of these schools of thought to explain in simple terms what I have discovered. Transcendental Meditation is a simple practice that allows the mind to settle down and access finer and finer levels of thought. With this practice, one can transcend or go beyond "thought" and soak in the source of "Pure Consciousness." (Sounds pretty cool, right? You don't have to believe it. It doesn't require faith. But an experience of "Pure Consciousness" can definitely increase one's "Faith.")

One of the best descriptions to answer this question about Transcendental Meditation is given in Maharishi Mahesh Yogis book *The Science of Being and Art of Living*, and it states the following:

"This book presents a practical thesis of integrated life which has long been the abstract goal of the various sciences, religions, and metaphysical thought groups. This thesis will enable all human beings to harmonize their inner spiritual content with the glories of the outer material life and find their God within themselves." (Mahesh Yogi, 1963)

I have come to believe that religions were created as the schools of thought enlightened beings tried to teach what they had learned about life and existence and God. I believe Jesus Christ, Buddha, Mohamad, Maharishi, Krishna, Hermes and Shiva were all spiritual teachers or enlightened beings trying to teach spiritual wisdom. Many of these spiritual teachers recognized the same fundamental aspects of reality but in different times and with different styles of language and different means of teaching those around them.

It's important not to let language or religion create a barrier for gaining more understanding. In the study of mathematics, there are many different types of math that can be used, including addition, subtraction, multiplication, division, and so on. We can't let pride restrict our minds and make us reluctant to understand other beliefs systems. Can we go beyond the limitation of our own beliefs?

I think God can talk to those who are willing and able to truly listen. It takes great strength of mind to be a man or woman of God. To know the truth, one must let go of opinion.

Are You Going to Try and Convert Me to Your Beliefs?

I'm only going to point you in the direction of self-reflection. Once we become more self-reflective, we will see and know the truth. With continued practice over time, we will spontaneously self-correct any limiting beliefs we may hold that prevent us from evolving further and which instead will allow us to self-direct our character in this game we call life.

What?

Just relax! We all learn and grow at different paces. Look at the trees. Some are small and have a lot of growing to do. Some are already big and tall. Life is a learning process! Don't compare your Self to other trees'. Just keep growing your Self.

The best way to keep an open mind and process objective knowledge is the practice of Transcendental Meditation. Imagine two empty cups and a bottle of water. One cup is face up, the other is face down. The cup that is face up represents an open mind. The cup that is face down represents a closed mind. Out of these two cups, which one will be more likely to receive and retain the water you try to pour into it?

The way the cup that is face up will receive and retain the water is the same way an open mind will be able to receive and retain knowledge. Transcendental Meditation is a practical way to open the mind to receive and retain knowledge. Transcendental Meditation is also a way to process, integrate, discern, and apply knowledge.

Whether you learn it or not is up to you. I recommend learning Transcendental Meditation as soon as possible in your life. I wish I'd learned it when I was 13 years old because it would probably have allowed me to find peace within myself instead of searching for it in drugs and alcohol. It would have allowed me to utilize my mind at a younger age and work more effectively and efficiently at identifying my goals and pursuing them instead of doubting myself and living a limited life. If you don't want to learn Transcendental Meditation that is okay. Keep reading and consider it later. But it is the step that will make all other steps seem more effortless.

STEP 2:
LEARN TRANSCENDENTAL MEDITATION

Self-reflection, self-correction, self-direction

DUSTIN MATTHEWS (TO BE DETERMINED)

To learn more about Transcendental Meditation go to www.tm.org.

Natural Laws or Hermetic Principles

What are Natural Laws?

Natural Laws are the laws of Nature, not the laws that are created by men and women. Natural laws. Laws of the Universe. The Hermetic Principles. All different labels for the same fundamental constructs of reality.

Hermes Trismegistus is thought to be the author of the *Emerald Tablet* and the *Corpus Hermeticum*. He is the author known as the Egyptian God Thoth and the Greek God Hermes, who were both considered gods of writing and magic in their cultures. The 7 Hermetic Principles were written as a way for individuals to understand the deeper levels of reality. (*Three Initiates*, 1908)

They consist of the following:

- The Law of Mentalism or Pure Potentiality

- The Law of Correspondence

- The Law of Attraction or Vibration

- The Law of Polarity

- The Law of Rhythm

- The Law of Cause and Effect

- The Law of Gender

The Law of Mentalism or Pure Potentiality

"This Principle embodies the truth that 'All is Mind.' It explains that THE ALL (which is the Substantial Reality underlying all the outward manifestations and appearances which we know under the terms of 'The Material Universe'; the 'Phenomena of Life'; 'Matter'; 'Energy'; and in short, all that is apparent to our material senses) is SPIRIT, which in itself is UNKNOWABLE and UNDEFINABLE, but which may be considered and thought of as AN UNIVERSAL, INFINITE, LIVING MIND." (*Three Initiates*, 1908, pg.26)

So, the ALL MIND, The Universe, Thy Self, God, Pure Consciousness, Atma Brahm, Individual Soul is the Total Soul. This is the understanding that everything is within The ALL. In words more familiar to new-age thinkers and modern scientists. Consciousness is primary. It's all a matter of perception. The unified field. "Aham Brahmasmi" in Vedic literature means, "I am Totality." And we are all tapped in and part of the ALL MIND.

I will discuss further how through the practice of Transcendental Meditation one can discover and experience the limitless potential of the mind and better understand this law, the Universe, Thy Self, God, and Consciousness. I will share some experiences that have validated the Law of Mentalism or Pure Potentiality for me personally.

When I played college football, I'd "imagine" or "visualize" running through plays in my head, making great blocks, big runs, good catches, and scoring touchdowns. One of my favorite movies at the time was *Gladiator*. My favorite part was when Maximus battled it out with a bunch of others who were all against him. He slaughtered them all in a seemingly impossible victory and then threw his sword into the crowd. The crowd went silent and Maximus yelled, "Are you not entertained?" with his arms outstretched. "Are you not entertained? Is this not why you are here?" *Awesome!* I thought.

How does this relate? For years, I visualized scoring a touchdown and holding my arms out to my sides in the end zone and yelling, "Are you not entertained?" During the last game of my college football career, I caught a touchdown pass in the fourth quarter and stood holding the ball with my arms outstretched and thought this is it, "Are you not entertained?" I made this happen. I imagined it for years after having surgery and being told I'd never play again and then it happened. To add to that, somehow a photographer snapped a picture of that moment, which I have as a reminder to my Self that I have the power to manifest things into my reality.

Another situation that increased my "faith" and understanding of the Law of Mentalism or Pure Potentiality was a few years ago when I lived in Fairfield, Iowa, and was getting my degree in Maharishi's Vedic Science, working on writing and recording music. I'd had a dream where I heard someone rapping really fast, and then I saw a hallway with a bunch of doors. In the dream, I was aware it was a dream and innocently observed but had no control over it. When I woke up, I'd completely forgotten the words, which was kind of sad because the lyrics had sounded really good.

About a week later, I was in the studio recording with a friend from school and we had just finished recording a song I wrote about "Cosmic Consciousness" or the feeling of being in the flow or an instrument of the Divine called, *Semi-Automatic*. We'd been recording for a few hours and I was tired, so I decided to meditate. I was on one side of the recording studio and my friend was on the other with a soundproof wall between us. I was sitting in the dark meditating for about fifteen minutes when I suddenly felt my breath pulled upward and instantly straightened me up in my chair.

I felt a connection through the top of my head and my eyes rolled back and it felt like the entire universe was within my own mind. I felt a very vast expansive presence of a guardian angel or warrior spirit above/inside/behind me. My breath was suspended, not breathing in or out. This Is It, I thought.

Time seemed to stand still, but in my mind's eye, I saw flashes of memories, which gave me a better understanding about why I'd done all the things in my life up to that point. I realized that I had to experience those things in order to teach others and share my experiences. And it was my voice that I'd heard in the dream a week earlier and I'd just recorded that song even though I thought I'd forgotten the lyrics. It was me in the dream, whom I'd heard, and I had somehow remembered the words and recorded that song anyway.

In that state, it felt like every intention of a thought I had was being answered by God instantly. Again, I call *It* God because *It* felt like a much higher power than myself. The range of emotions during this experience was complete fullness, happiness, and sadness all rolled into one. I saw all sides of my life, light and dark, good and bad, all rolled into one. I felt it All with every thought.

After what seemed like a few minutes, my breath came back into my body. I was laughing and crying simultaneously. I didn't know what to think. The experience was without the use of any drugs or substances. I walked out into the room and saw my friend and tried to explain it to him. We hugged each other and I was still laughing and crying. I then walked out into the hallway to calm myself.

As soon as I walked into the hallway, I realized it was the same hallway as in the dream and I began laughing and crying again. Goosebumps rose on my skin as I walked down the hallway in amazement. I'd seen all of this in the dream a week before, but I had no idea what it meant.

What it means to me now is that we are always being guided in our lives. Have Faith and continue to seek the Truth. You will be shown in time, what you need, when you need it.

Have you ever had an experience that you can't explain, but you know was real? Have you ever had a magical or mysterious experience that helped lead you to something better in your life? Take a moment to reflect and see what you recall in the text box below.

What are some examples of The Law of Mentalism or Pure Potential from your experience?

(Dustin Matthews, Plymouth State University, 2012)

The Law of Correspondence

"As above, so below; as below, so above. As within, so without; as without, so within."

-THE KYBALION

This Law states that there is always a correspondence between the laws and phenomena of the various planes of Being and Life (*Three Initiates*, 1908). In other words, there is an interconnectedness between all layers of existence from our outer world of matter, to our inner world of mind. By gaining a deeper understanding of this law, we can start to recognize the patterns in all aspects of Being and Life. Through introspection and self-reflection, we can start to see how our inner world or state of being is projected into the outer world. If we are at peace with ourselves, we can project that and help others find peace. If we are at war with ourselves, that can and usually does come out in ways that are harmful or destructive to ourselves and others.

With advances in modern scientific studies today, we are able to see things at finer levels, and quantum physicists have even discovered what they call the Unified Field. This Unified Field Theory supports the perspective that there is an underlying source of unity in all aspects of creation from the quantum to the cosmic. And we, as human beings, are part of this Unified Field.

"Modern science over the last 50 years has revealed that our physical universe is structured in layers of creation. This inward exploration is explored in four different parts, from outside in. Classical Mechanics is the study of the world of macroscopic objects that we can see. Quantum Mechanics is the discovery of the atom. Deeper than the atom is the atomic nucleus and sub nuclear particles, called Quantum Field Theory. Finally, the recent discovery of Unified Field Theories" (Hagelin, 2019).

PHYSICS   CONSCIOUSNESS

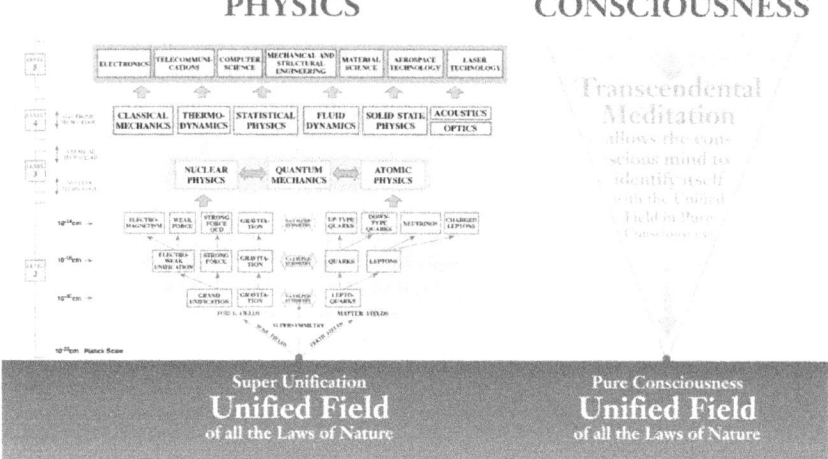

Note. Reprinted from Consciousness is the Unified Field – quantum physicist John Hagelin. (October 25, 2016) Retrieved from: https://transcendentalmeditationblog. wordpress.com/2016/10/25/consciousness-is-the-unified-field-quantum-physicist-john-hagelin/

The diagram above illustrates that the deepest layer, Unified Field Theories or super string theories, reveal the fundamental unity of life. "They show that at the basis of our diverse universe is a single universal field of intelligence—the fountainhead of all the laws of nature, and the source of all order displayed throughout the universe" (Hagelin, 2019).

This diagram is a great depiction of the Law of Correspondence. It demonstrates the interconnectedness of all things from the most subtle to the grossest layers of existence and how it all comes from the same source. It is a wonderful advancement in science and technology to bring us closer to the true constructs of our universe and reality and how individuals can experience the source of all the Laws of Nature within their own selves.

The Law of Attraction or Vibration

This law states that everything is energy and vibrates with a certain frequency (*Three Initiates*, 1908). Thoughts and feelings all have certain vibrations, which resonate at a certain frequency. Have you ever felt a positive or negative mood? Good or bad vibes? It's quantum physics, not just hippie nonsense.

And guess what? You attract the energy that you are mentally/emotionally transmitting. If you dwell on negative thoughts, then that is what you will feel and manifest into your reality. If you constantly focus on the negative and never find a solution or transform and transmute that energy into something positive, then don't expect to see different results.

Your mind and heart are the tools that consciously or unconsciously create, transmit, amplify, and attract whatever it is you think/feel about most deeply, most often. This scared me at first because I had a lot of negative thoughts and feelings, which would pop up, some of which manifested out of fear and an unconscious understanding of how these laws really work.

Fortunately, meditation helped me tremendously with purifying my heart and mind, so I no longer manifest negative things into my life unconsciously. I recognize, looking back, that this law is true whether you have good or bad thoughts, which is why Transcendental Meditation is Step 2. Because it will naturally and effortlessly help you understand your thought processes and the connection between your thoughts and feelings and what manifests into your life.

As I have grown in understanding, I've developed a more conscious awareness of the potential of my thoughts. I have also realized how this law has helped me understand the power of belief. I've had experiences that I now consider "Faith Builders." On my journey of "Self-Discovery," I've had the opportunity to discuss this type of knowledge with many people with different beliefs and backgrounds.

I've talked to preachers, teachers, friends, and even random strangers, and somehow, many of these interactions led me to a better understanding of what I was looking for. I was attracting the knowledge I was seeking.

Ask and it shall be given to you; seek and you will find; knock and the door will be opened to you.

-MATTHEW 7.7

I have learned that through the process of mind refinement or meditation, an individual can experience this "Pure Potentiality" or "Pure Consciousness" on a regular basis. The steps in this book deliver an understanding of this knowledge for you to gain and experience for your Self firsthand if you choose.

So how do you change your thoughts and attract positive things? Transcendental Meditation.

Why?

Many of us have learned from limiting perspectives and have had our minds conditioned to believe a certain viewpoint. There is no fault or blame for this; it is just how it is. Throughout time, our society or culture grows accustomed to a certain way of life and if our way of life is not harmonious with our own Nature, we can lose touch with our souls or our inner selves, which is what I believe to be the root cause of suffering.

For example, there is energy and there is matter. Matter is the material world. Energy is the spiritual world. However, energy cannot be created or destroyed. Matter on the other hand can be. It is in the transmutation of energy that attracts or repels materials.

Take an atom for example, which is the building block of matter. The atom consists of the nucleus and the protons and neutrons orbiting the nucleus. But the energy within the atom can only be perceived. Your perception is your energy. Your consciousness is your energy. Your power of awareness is your energy. Your energy is your soul or spirit. This is how you can learn to consciously be aware of your energy and what you are attracting.

You are not your mind. You are not your body. You are "Consciousness". Where you choose to put your "Conscious Awareness" is what will manifest into your reality. For some, it may happen instantaneously; for others, it may take more time. The more refined your mind and physiology, the easier it will be to understand and manifest more positive things in your life.

Some more concrete or practical methods to manifesting the things you desire can come from visualization practices. Later, I will discuss some things you can practice to help attract the positive things you desire. Visualizing the things or experiences you wish for can help attract them into your physical reality. But it takes practice, effort, and energy.

I feel like the biggest reason people give up when trying to manifest things into their life it is because they lack the patience to continue having faith when obstacles arise. They surrender their true goals and dreams for instant gratification. I know it can be hard to have patience and faith. One thing that helps the most is to find your reason *why*; more on this later, too.

The Law of Polarity

This is the law of opposites. "Everything is dual" (*Kybalion*, 1908, pg. 32). Everything has a pair of opposites measured or expressed to a different degree or extreme. Hot and cold are both measured in degrees but are two opposite extremes. Up and down, in and out, left and right, north and south, east and west. Without one, we wouldn't have the other. Imagine a scale with all of the extremes on one side and each of these extremes' polar opposite on the other side (*Three Initiates*, 1908).

These extremes are all on different ends of the same scale. Left and right come together to meet in the middle. Extremism is not balance. It takes a balanced, stable-minded individual to see from both perspectives.

So how do we keep from getting sucked into extreme viewpoints, thoughts, or emotions?

With the practice of meditation, you can start to gain a deeper sense of equanimity and balance. By refining your mind and understanding these laws, you can maintain a certain level of stability, which will allow you to rise above negativity. By becoming more "Consciously Aware" of how to work with these laws, you will recognize those things in your life that are negative and eliminate or transmute them into a positive direction.

It's All within You.

Some say the grass is always greener on the other side. Now, imagine a fence in the middle of those two yards of green grass. Imagine you are sitting on top of the fence and are able to see both sides of the two different yards of green grass for what they really are and not what you imagine them to be. Seeing multiple perspectives from a point of neutrality can help us make the best, most balanced decisions. Now imagine the scale of polarity is like a seesaw. Sitting on either side will not bring balance but sitting in the middle will allow you to see both perspectives and explain to others who are on the extreme ends of some scales in life to see from a more balanced, fair-minded, harmonious perspective. Meditating can help reestablish balance and understanding of polar opposites.

Peace cannot be kept by force; it can only be achieved
by understanding.

-ALBERT EINSTEIN

SOCIAL CONDITIONING & DUALITY

Good or Socially Acceptable	Bad or Socially Unacceptable
• Rich	• Poor
• Healthy	• Unhealthy
• Nice	• Mean
• Intelligent	• Ignorant
• Order	• Chaos
• Right	• Wrong
• Light	• Dark
• Conscious	• Unconscious
• Ego	• Shadow

The image and table above depict and categorize the polarities we see in society today. Our social conditioning teaches us to behave in a certain way or ascertain certain qualities while rejecting other qualities, which can create a stigma of intolerance or repression of certain parts of our own selves or members of our society. For example, if we are raised and taught from a young age that money is a good thing and being poor is bad, this can lead to many issues but one being the mistreatment of poor people because we classify them as bad. In reality, we all contain these character traits individually and collectively, and for the most part, I think as a civilization, we try our best to stick to the "Good" category. However, recognizing the Unity in the Diversity is the Totality. All of the Laws of Nature work together to create and restore balance. That is what these images represent. The duality/polarity and unifying balance of the extremes. It is important to understand this so we can restore balance and neutralize the extreme polarization, which is what causes imbalance. How can we restore balance (individually and collectively)?

WHAT QUALITIES/CHARACTERISTICS WOULD UNIFY THESE TWO POLAR OPPOSITES?

Good or Socially Acceptable	The Great Unifier	Bad or Socially Unacceptable
• Rich	• Generosity	• Poor
• Healthy	• Health Care	• Unhealthy
• Nice	• Kindness/Compassion/Empathy	• Mean
• Intelligent	• Education/Knowledge	• Ignorant
• Order	• Structure/Support	• Chaos
• Right	• Education/Justice/Reform	• Wrong
• Light	• Acceptance/Free Will	• Dark
• Conscious	• Increased Awareness	• Unconscious
• Ego	• Integration	• Shadow

The table above is an example I filled out with what I thought would be the qualities or character traits to unify the extremes. I think the primary traits that will overlap into all areas are acceptance, empathy, knowledge, and awareness. Recognizing and accepting that there will always be outliers on both ends of the spectrum and learning to have empathy for both sides is key. In order to maintain balance, we gain/share knowledge and increase awareness.

The Law of Rhythm

This law states that everything flows or orbits. The planets rotate around the Sun on an orbit. That is why we have day and night. Tides ebb and flow in and out with the ocean. What goes up must come down. Working with the Law of Polarity, the Law of Rhythm swings back and forth on the pendulum of duality (*Three Initiates*, 1908).

It is wise to seek balance and moderation. Try to remember that if things are down, they will get better, and be grateful for the good things you do have right now. Become in tune with the Rhythm of Nature. Align your Self with the Laws of Nature. Life will teach you about balance. Wake and sleep with the rise and setting of the sun.

Take the ups and downs of experiencing life with equanimity, through loss and gain, love and pain. An analogy for this is "Surfing." Life can throw some big waves at you but learning to meditate can be like learning to surf. At first, those waves might crash down on you and you might feel like you're drowning. But with the proper tool "a surfboard" or "Transcendental Meditation," you can learn to ride the waves life throws at you and go with the flow rather than fight against the waves. Meditation is a way to neutralize the extremes and balance the scales.

My experience with rhythm, the reason that I'm still living,

My soul is so in the flow I do what my mind envisions.

I write about life lessons, I'm learning from my depression,

So low, I've been so high, now finally I get the message.

I'm riding out with the tide,

I focus my higher mind,

I'm living, I'm loving, laughing,

I'm guided by God inside.

DUSTIN MATTHEWS (TO BE DETERMINED)

So, go with the flow. Accept change. Change is constant. Learn to adapt and integrate what you've learned to continue to progress. What is unchanging and eternal within your body and mind is your soul or consciousness.

The Law of Cause and Effect

"There is a Cause for every Effect; an Effect from every Cause" (*Kybalion*, 1908, pg. 38). In the Vedic tradition, the word "karma" means "action," and all actions have consequences. Some causes have greater effects just like some actions have greater consequences. Good or bad. An example of this law can be seen in the justice system. Let's say you're late for work, which causes the action of speeding, the effects of the action can be varied.

Sometimes, the potential outcome of an action can be calculated by the mind, as thus: "Okay, I'm late and I'm going 10 miles per hour over the speed limit. That could cause a small speeding ticket or a warning if I get pulled over." Or "Okay, I'm going 30 miles per hour over the speed limit, which is potentially more dangerous to others and will probably cause a more expensive ticket if not a more severe punishment, like criminal speeding and loss of my driver's license."

This is then a calculated risk by the subject. They can choose the action, but they don't have complete control over the effect. As you grow in this understanding, you can develop the ability to foresee or simulate experiences in your mind to see where certain actions might lead and have the conscious ability to avoid taking actions (cause) that could lead to negative outcomes (effect). But try not to get too caught up in trying to see the outcome of every situation because this can cause indecision.

You have a right to perform your prescribed duties, but you are not entitled to the fruits of your actions. Never consider yourself to be the cause of the results of your activities, nor be attached to inaction.

-BHAGAVAD GITA, CH. 2. V. 47

I have spent a long time contemplating this quote and believe it relates to not getting so caught up in how things might turn out. Instead, just try to do your best with good intentions, good thoughts, good actions, and pray for good results. But no matter what results from your actions, try not to blame your Self if they are not as good as you'd hoped for; if the results are good, be grateful to have received that blessing. If the results are not good, accept and forgive because those were the results of karma. The best thing we can do is learn from it and move forward.

All these laws work together simultaneously. Understanding the Law of Mentalism or Pure Potential and the Law of Attraction can aid in your decision-making skills. The simplest way to explain this so you can understand the magnitude of it is this:

"Watch your thoughts, they become your words; watch your words, they become your actions; watch your actions, they become your habits; watch your habits, they become your character; watch your character, it becomes your destiny."

-LAO TZU

But what comes before thought? Being. *Is*-ness. Pure Consciousness. The ALL Mind. Meditating can help bring clarity to the importance of understanding the Law of Mentalism or Pure Potentiality. Every Action has a Consequence. Think good thoughts, do good things, and good things will start happening ... eventually. You may still have to deal with the karma you've accumulated over the course of time. But that can be done by expanding our "Conscious Awareness."

Another analogy to try to better grasp the law of cause and effect: If you throw a boomerang, it will go out a distance and come back to you. Your thoughts and actions in this world will have a boomerang effect on you. What you put out into the world will come back to you. Do good, and good will happen to you. And remember you can neutralize negativity through the practice of meditation.

The Law of Gender

This law states that both the masculine and feminine exist in all things. Not just on the basis of biological sex but also in the nature of all things on all planes of existence: the physical, mental, and spiritual planes (*Three Initiates*, 1908). The character traits of the masculine are assertive, progressive, penetrative, and explorative energies that drive progress. The character traits of the feminine are the receptive, sacred, nurturing, protective energies that maintain what is most essential to life. Simply put, masculine is doing; feminine is being.

Too much masculine energy leads to an abuse of power to the extremes of tyranny, greed, overindulgence, destruction, and injustice. This type of imbalance can cause us to lose perspective on what principles are most important. Too much feminine energy leads to a life of complacency and contempt where our lives become determined too strongly by outside forces.

All beings contain these two parts within themselves. Every male has both masculine energy and feminine energy, and every female has both feminine energy and masculine energy. We can see the interplay of these energies within ourselves through our moods, actions, attitudes, and personalities. We can also start to see the effects of these energies in our society as a whole.

In order to restore balance, we must first look within ourselves and gain a deeper understanding of our own nature to be part of the sustainable solution in our families, communities, and the world at large. This can be done by self-reflection (or Transcendental Meditation). Ask yourself: How present am I in my daily life? Am I future-oriented? What have I sacrificed to reach my goals? What's most important to me? How much do I give? How much do I receive? How much do I speak? How much do I listen? Am I balanced in my own masculine and feminine energies?

How to Live in Harmony with the Laws of Nature

In order to live in harmony with the Laws of Nature or the Laws of the Universe, you need access to the "Right Knowledge" and a practical way to apply it. The reason some people are unsuccessful, unhappy, and unfulfilled is because they have not discovered the "Right Knowledge." And not having access to the "Right Knowledge" can leave people feeling unsatisfied, unmotivated, anxious, depressed, sad, angry, and confused.

On the outside, I faired pretty well in the general educational system I grew up in. Good grades, athletic, smart, funny, and dangerously good looking. But I was also depressed, angry, sad, and searching for something I didn't even know I was looking for. It took me twenty-four years to find the "Right Knowledge." And eventually, I hope all education has its foundation in human development or consciousness-based education. The "Right Knowledge" is "Subjective Knowledge". Connection with the ALL mind or spirit. Whatever you want to call It, It Is. Transcendental Meditation is the practical application I found to help strengthen my connection with God/The ALL Mind/Pure Consciousness/My Higher Self. And you can too.

The "Right Knowledge" and Application

There is so much objective knowledge and information in the world today, it seems endless. Diets, exercise routines, so many numbers, figures, languages, concepts, religions, financial investments, business opportunities, self-help books, and so on.

I have three degrees and have spent years trying to educate my Self in an effort to figure it all out. Now I'm writing a book to help others evolve and learn what I found to be the most beneficial in this process we call life. So, I will attempt to deliver the "Right Knowledge" as quickly as possible and share some ways you can apply it.

So, what is the "Right Knowledge?" Self-knowledge. Subjective knowledge. You yourself are the subject. The "Right Knowledge" can be discovered through the practice of meditation. By reading this book, you have found a drop of "Right Knowledge."

If you meditate regularly, you will be led to the ocean of "All Knowledge", which has the power to realign your mind to "right thinking" and eventually "right doing." Try it out for yourself.

It's a process. Like life. You will see, in time, "all possibilities." But stick to it. Results might not happen overnight. Be patient. Be persistent. Be kind.

Some other easy and practical ways to learn more about the Laws of Nature is to spend more time in Nature. Observe Nature. Observe your Self.

Know Thyself

-PAUSANIAS

This simple quote has been interpreted and studied by many great minds throughout history. I believe it is essential for a person to know who he/she truly is to be content/fulfilled/successful/happy. Sometimes, in the world we live in today, we can be distracted and confronted by things that *mislead us,* these things are usually ego-driven. If we get to know and learn to believe in ourselves, then we will have the courage to act from a "Higher State of Consciousness," and petty desires will start to fall away. Also, understand when I say, Self, I am talking about the most fundamental aspect of your Being. Some call it the "Soul" or "Spirit," while others may call it "Consciousness." I believe they are All One.

The quote above is interpreted differently by everyone because we all have our own minds, bodies, individual souls, personalities, beliefs, values, and so on. Everyone has their own perceptions, thoughts, feelings, and life experiences, so, the learning process will be different for everybody. However, we are all fundamentally very similar. We are all living beings; we are all self-conscious beings. If we were not self-conscious beings, how could you be reading this book and thinking these thoughts?

Unfortunately, it seems that not enough people in the world today recognize this most fundamental aspect of who we truly are. And this is called "Maya" or ignorance, which is the root cause for all suffering including but not limited to stress, depression, anxiety, loneliness, drug abuse, alcoholism, corruption, corporate greed, lack of education, and so on. Therefore, it is crucial to take some personal time and get to know that deeper part of who you really are. Why do we think, feel, and act the way that we do? Is every experience we have really perceived through a lens colored by our emotional responses from past experiences? Does the human brain really have the potential to be programmed so we act in ways that we don't understand? Is there a secret key to unlocking the brain so we can discover the mysteries of the Universe? Yes.

According to Dr. Fred Travis' book *Your Brain Is a River Not a Rock,* the brain is constantly changing and making new neural connections, which is why the title of the book is an analogy for the brain's neuroplasticity. This means every day we wake up our brain is structured differently than the day before. We are constantly having new experiences, which are leaving new impressions on our brains. However, the impressions left on our brains from past experiences can sometimes still affect how we perceive new experiences. This happens when our sensory system receives stimulus from a new experience, and the part of our brain that deals with emotions and memories colors that new experience, based on our previous life experiences.

That means that every experience we have is being perceived from a tinted perspective based on our previous experiences. This is why some people may have experiences that "trigger" old feelings or cause explosive behavior. This process of how the brain experiences reality is what Dr. Travis calls the "high road/low road response." The "low road response" is the unconscious reaction of the part of our brain (amygdala) responding to past experiences that may be triggering old memories or emotions. The "high road response" is recognizing this in your "Conscious Awareness" (prefrontal cortex) so that you will recognize the old pattern or lens and then have a choice to see things differently. The prefrontal cortex or your "Conscious Awareness" is the decision-making center of the brain. But our feeling brain is what usually drives our behavior if we are unconscious of our emotional responses. (Travis, 2012)

Now that we have the awareness of the "low road" past experiences and the "high road," which enables the "Conscious Awareness" to see both perspectives, our Consciousness can expand. In order to grow more "Consciously Aware" of the thoughts, feelings, and behaviors or actions we consciously or unconsciously choose, we should continue applying the steps in this book and reflecting as we do so. By doing these things, you will start to gain more clarity and awareness of our own thoughts, feelings, and behaviors and start to have the "Conscious Awareness" to recognize your own thought patterns, habits, and emotional responses.

When learning more about this fundamental aspect of who you really are and how you function, you will gain a better understanding of why you do the things you do. You will recognize patterns of thoughts, feelings, and behavior and realize there is a choice in everything that you do or don't do. You will start to free yourself from the chains of your own mind by recognizing or becoming more "Consciously Aware" of your "unconscious emotional responses." This is one of the benefits of being on the path to self-knowledge. You can free your Self from suffering.

I have found this path to self-knowledge the most fulfilling form of any knowledge because it is the key to unlocking all knowledge and possibilities and freeing oneself from any pain or suffering. Although it can be a lonely path, it is a path we can choose. When we choose to go down the path of self-knowledge and accept who we are in our own selves we will begin to discover and understand more and more.

On my path to self-knowledge, I tried a lot of different things at first. I read all kinds of self-help books. I took a personality test. I read about meditation, religion, and astrology. And eventually, all my studies led me to the source. I just want you to learn faster than I did. It took me thirty years to accumulate the knowledge and understanding I have now and maybe even longer if I had past lives, but I want you to have access to what I believe is the "Right Knowledge" and the steps you can take to apply it in your life.

Be without the three gunas, Oh Arjuna.

-BHAGAVAD GITA

What's a guna? Guna is a sankrit word for "quality" or "attribute" and the three gunas represent the three forces of nature that uphold activity. These three gunas are called: sattva (goodness, constructive, harmonious), rajas (passion, active, confused), and tamas (darkness, destructive, chaotic). Being without the three gunas means to transcend. Transcendental Meditation can help you understand this thought a little more clearly because it will allow you the experience of "going beyond" these forces of nature.

Life

Life is a constantly evolving co-creative process. A human is birthed from a man and woman through the process of sexual reproduction. An egg and a seed. Sexual reproduction causes the growth and further reproduction of cells over a period of time evolving into matter and then a baby is born. The baby then evolves into a child, a teen, a young adult, an adult, and an elder, and then the physical body dies.

Throughout the life cycle of that individual, he/she will be molded by his/her subjective or personal experiences, thoughts, and beliefs. However, these experiences, thoughts, and beliefs need to be properly understood by the individual in order to learn and continue to evolve. If someone goes their entire life absorbing the many mixed messages that society sends today, then it is no wonder that there is so much suffering. Learning to integrate experiences, thoughts, and beliefs more efficiently, will allow individuals to live a more conscious, intelligent, healthier, happier, Self-Directed life.

With the continued practice of Transcendental Meditation, you can begin to experience a silencing of the mind and even live in "Higher States of Consciousness." The silencing of the mind leads to a state of consciousness called "Pure Consciousness." Within this state of "Pure Consciousness," it is possible to access all knowledge, which helps the individual to more effectively integrate past experiences, thoughts, and beliefs to benefit his/her own individual growth and evolution naturally. It isn't always something that needs to be done intellectually.

The practice of Transcendental Meditation is completely subjective in terms of experience. From my personal experience, it has helped me stay clean and sober for more than seven years. It allowed me to integrate and understand many of my past experiences as stepping-stones, teaching me along the way. It has also allowed me to foresee how certain actions could possibly play out. It has supplied me with an infinite supply of creativity and the discernment necessary to prioritize my life and choose which decisions are in the best interest of my Self and the collective as a whole. And most importantly it brings me peace, silence and stillness.

My Experience of the Illusion of Death

I live in this body but what happens when my body dies? I believe that the moment my body dies, my breath leaves my body, and then I realize my breath is my soul or consciousness and that is what is living through this body. My breath then becomes free and completely expands throughout the entire universe realizing All is One. This is the point of complete wholeness and freedom from any limiting physical form. Free of any desire. You are All that Is. Infinite. Death is not the end.

From this expansion of perspective either at death or in a transcendental state of consciousness, it's possible to see and understand why things happened in your life the way they did. You see from all perspectives, not only from your individual perspective held within your own body and mind. You're able to understand everything with the slightest of intentions. You see how other people saw you. You realize how important your presence was to others. You see why you lived and what your purpose was. You're pure. There is no more need for selfishness or egocentricity. You forgive yourself and others. You're happy and content with the life you've lived. You've left your human senses behind but still have the potential to feel, hear, see, taste, smell, and touch. Would you like to come back to life? What would you say? What would you do? How would you act? How would you explain that to people? God? The magnificence and beauty of this is beyond form. But you can try your best to let others know. This type of experience came to me as a glimpse of "Parinirvana" or nirvana after death.

How do I know? Subjective experience. I accept what Is. I have faith. I trust. I Love. My experiences have taught me this. There is nothing to fear. Breathe. This is life. It is a cycle. Breathe in, breathe out. Live free from the fear of death. Do all you wish to do. Bring this to your awareness and remember your life is a choice.

My advice: Meditate, pray, surrender, set intentions, educate yourself, work, keep learning, be persistent, be patient, be kind, speak the truth, and Love.

Communication

We must learn to communicate effectively and efficiently. Precise and concise communication provides clarity through simplicity. There are two parts to communication—that which is said and that which is heard. Therefore, we must be able to listen with an open mind and compassionate heart and try to understand and empathize with others.

Be an active listener. Engage with the person you are communicating with. Eye contact is important for the most beneficial in-person communication. Be honest. If communication becomes difficult due to intense emotions, remember to breathe deeply and think before you speak.

- Listen carefully.

- Act; do not react.

- Check for understanding.

- Repeat things back to the person to make sure you understood correctly.

- Silence or Conscious Awareness is the best tool for effective communication. The majority of communication is nonverbal. There's more being communicated than what someone's saying.

- Be consciously aware.

- Be consciously aware of your energy and others energy.

- Be consciously aware of your body language and others body language.

In order to make peace with others, we must find it within ourselves.

-DUSTIN MATTHEWS (TO BE DETERMINED)

The Art of Effective Communication

Why are you communicating? Purpose of Communication. Reason for Communication.

The purpose for this section on communication is to educate others on the fundamentals of what communication is and how to improve your ability to communicate more efficiently and more effectively. The reason I want to share this knowledge is because my experiences have led me to believe that communication is a key component in many areas of life. Communication is a way to connect with others. It is like a bridge between people that helps them connect.

There are numerous benefits to increasing our knowledge on effective and efficient communication. Communication is an exchange of energy on a subtle level. It is the exchange of objective information or ideas, the exchange of emotions or subjective experiences.

It is my understanding that communication is a way of verbalizing thought. The definition of a verb is an action word. So, communication comes from thought. Thoughts can sometimes be unorganized, abstract, chaotic, and ever changing depending on your emotional state or experiences.

Why is this important? Because with certain practices, you can better understand the process of your thoughts allowing for a more effective, coherent, and organized style of communication.

If we can develop a better understanding of the actual process of communication, we will be more effective and efficient in all areas of life. Personal and professional. It all starts within you.

How?

"How" explains the process of communication in its many forms.

How is it being expressed?

It comes from Thought. What is the Source of Thought? The Unified Field? God?

How are your thoughts expressed or communicated?

Feeling, emotion, writing, speaking, singing, rapping, art, dance, tone, tune, language, dialect, vocabulary, volume, body position, truth.

Many things come into play when communicating. The power of emotion used in communication can inspire or motivate or educate others. However, different styles of communication will speak to different people.

Some people learn best through clear, concise logical communication. Others may learn better through poetry or song or dance due to the emotional aspect. Some people even learn better by communicating with numbers like mathematicians. We're all different and operate more effectively with different styles of communication.

Different subject areas require different vocabulary, ideologies, or conceptual levels of thinking. Are you communicating in terms of numbers, words, or art?

These are all examples of how you communicate.

What?

What is the message?

It starts as a thought, idea, or concept and develops into form. This takes thought, silence, reflection, meditation, reading, and revising. Integration of knowledge and experience.

Listen first. Get the facts. Get the details. Get an understanding. Integrate what you've learned from your experiences. Then, communicate or express into form what you think needs to be said.

Effective communication requires intuitive, logical progressive forward thinking and the ability to adapt to how you communicate depending on the gap you're trying to bridge or the audience you're trying to reach.

Develop the ability to think on different levels. Communication is dependent on the language, age, maturity, intelligence, emotional intelligence, coherence, and willingness to learn by your audience.

In business. What is the market you're trying to reach? What is the problem that needs solving? The solution is what your service or product will provide?

- Ask the right questions

- Check for understanding

- Speak the truth

- Be clear and concise

- Understand that communicating is a skill and an art

The people I hope to reach are those trying to help themselves and develop as human beings. The problem that needs solving is "How to Develop Our Limitless Human Potential." The solution is in this book, which points you in the direction of a sequence of steps that will ultimately unlock the limitless power you possess within your Self.

- Develop your ability to listen/receive/retain information.

- Refine your perception to hear what is not being said.

- Learn to trust your intuition by asking the right questions. This can also be considered probing. Be compassionate of others and ask for consent if it's necessary.

- Remain calm. Probing and having difficult discussions can arouse emotions.

- Return to silence, balance. Integrate knowledge and experience. Apply what you have learned.

- Silence speaks.

- Go deeper than the surface.

- Get to the roots.

This may take time and effort, patience, and practice.

How to improve your communication skills?

- Meditation. Reading. Writing. Speaking.

- Think about thinking.

- Listen about listening.

- Read about reading.

- Write about writing.

- Talk about talking.

- Learn about learning.

This will allow you to better understand the process of the action itself, which will bring greater clarity and understanding of how these communication tools can be used more effectively.

Communication Styles

- **Analytical**—What are the facts? Give me the numbers: the cold, hard data-driven decision makers. This style can be productive if logical data-driven decisions need to be made. But it is not the most friendly or heartwarming style of communication. These people don't have time for feelings they're usually serious and driven by factual information. This is just an example of how analytical people communicate best with numbers and figures.

- **Intuitive**—These folks see and like the big picture but might not always "really" *get* the big picture. They enjoy speaking freely and are usually quick witted and fun. They speak openly and like to get to the point quickly. There is no need for this type of person to go into the details. These are people who like tarot cards and palm reading. To people with less trust in intuition or the unseen, these folks can seem untrusting and whimsical. How do they know? What's the process? What are the facts? Just listen to your heart.

- **Functional**—Let me take you step by step through the process of a functional communicator. I want you to understand just how my methodical robot mind works. 1.2.3. A.B.C. This and then that. Similar to analytical. Structured and organized thinking is the most logical approach to communication if you want people to be able to follow your thoughts and understand what you're trying to convey. This is necessary for herding sheep or getting people to follow directions. This book is semi-formatted in a functional way. But if you haven't figured it out yet, I'm intuitive and personal because I like knowledge to be fun.

- **Personal**—Let me tell you a story. I was giving a lecture a few weeks ago and I started the lecture with a joke. The audience laughed and I could feel the mood lighten up. It was a group of 100-plus computer science students, so I'm guessing they were mostly functional and analytical communicators. But who doesn't like a good joke? No matter what style of communicator you are, you're still a person and you still have feelings. And that's what I'm going to try and help you see as we dive deeper into *IMAGINE: The Simple Steps to Success.* Authenticity. Be yourself.

Success

"Success is really nothing more than the progressive realization of a worthy ideal."

-EARL NIGHTINGALE

If we have goals that we are working toward, then we are a success. We will become what we think about most often, most powerfully. So, try to think positively, realistically, progressively, and creatively. Products and services come before successes both in the dictionary and the world as we currently perceive it. So does effort, energy, and hard work.

Set a definite goal and focus on your goal every day. Create and follow your plan of action and keep meditating.

Distraction

Dictionary Definition

> *Distraction*: A thing that prevents someone from giving full attention to something else.

My Definition

> *Distraction*: Distancing ourselves from the track of action.

Eliminate all distractions. These come in many forms. Video games, TV, toxic relationships, parties, drugs, alcohol, negative thoughts. If you know what your kryptonite is, defeat it. Sometimes, we have to do what we have to do, in order to do what we love to do.

It's important to act like the person you want to be. We can change our self-image as easily as we change our perceptions of the world. Think of all the reasons you can be successful, and you will be.

> *Love your Self. Invest your time. Master your craft. Earn your keep.*
> *Live your dream. Save our world.*
>
> -DUSTIN MATTHEWS (TO BE DETERMINED)

Effort and Energy

So, everything is energy, and our thoughts can manifest into reality. But as thoughts come and go so often, it is a constant battle in our minds to concentrate on our awareness. Learning from the negative and focusing on the positive is good but control is not what you should be after. Learning to live from a state of Being is more like surrendering of the mind than it is control of the mind. Surrender to the "Higher Self" within you. The organizing intelligence of nature. Truth. Knowledge.

In the physical or material world today, much of human attention and energy is directed on gaining more physical possessions or acquiring a desirable physical appearance. It's out of balance. Although these physical or concrete things may enhance the quality of your life to a certain degree, overindulgence or obsession in these areas can lead to suffering. All matter is made of energy. Energy cannot be created or destroyed. But it can be redirected or transmuted.

I used to obsess about working out and gaining muscle in an effort to be the best athlete. I directed so much energy toward my physical performance that I ended up sacrificing my mental and emotional health. I suffered from numerous injuries and drug and alcohol abuse, depression, and anger issues. However, I was fortunate enough to learn to meditate and to redirect my energy toward something else—something that does not have a monetary value in the physical world but something that has more value to me personally. Spiritual Enlightenment. Happiness. Inner Peace.

"Effort and Energy" are contagious; think of it like Newton's First Law of Motion. An object in motion will stay in motion unless acted upon by an outside force. The same is true for "thinking and energy." If you are stuck in negative thinking, it is up to your "Conscious Mind" to change that by eliminating negative thoughts and redirecting your energy in a positive direction. It is important to learn to observe your own energy and try to affect others in a positive way. We can learn how to access a field of "Pure Consciousness" through the process of Transcendental Meditation, which can increase our capacity to think and act with more energy, more effectively. (Mahesh Yogi, 1963)

Thinking positively comes from a state of Being. If you find yourself thinking negatively or being affected by those who are negative, it is up to you to realize this and then accept it—leave it or try to change it. Transcendental Meditation is a great way to help you cultivate a state of mind that will begin to spontaneously act in ways that diffuse negative situations and provide clarity and understanding. It's hard to give specific advice because different circumstances require different actions or words of wisdom. But …

patience and compassion help. Listen and ask questions. Be humble and kind. Listen to your "Higher Self". What resonates with the Truth in your heart?

When you are able to quiet your mind, you can start to better understand the process of your own thoughts. In summary, as your mind becomes quieter and quieter you connect to a deeper part of your own mind until you reach the source of thought—"Pure Consciousness." Contacting the source of thought is like the key to unlock any door. With the steady practice of Transcendental Meditation, one can operate from the field of "Pure Consciousness" even in activity.

The mind can transform and become a superconductor that is not affected by outside influences and is steady and stable in itself. This will allow better control of your own senses and free you from the habitual patterns of negative thinking, feeling, or behaviors you may have suffered from before. This allows you to begin thinking more positively over time by soaking in the source of "Pure Consciousness" also known as the "field of all possibilities" or the "Absolute" (Mahesh Yogi, 1963). The more time you spend here, the more stress dissolves until you are filled with the "Absolute" resulting in greater peace and happiness all the time.

When the conscious mind expands to embrace deeper levels of thinking, the thought waves become more powerful and results in added energy and intelligence.

-MAHARISHI MAHESH YOGI

Direct your effort and energy. Obstacles or temptations will arise in meditation just as they may arise in your physical life. These obstacles or temptations are forms of energy. Some can be eliminated right away but some have accumulated more mass and will take more time and effort and conscious energy to dissolve. Someday, you may hear someone say, "Be easy and take it as it comes."

The following lists some of these obstacles or temptations and how to eliminate them.

Obstacles or Temptations

"The following five states are likely to prevent or block the success of our efforts to lead the upright life of a Buddhist lay follower. They are called by the Buddha the five mental hindrances *(pañcanivarana)* because they close the doors to both spiritual and worldly progress. Although the Buddha originally taught them as the main obstacles to meditation, with a little reflection we can see that they are equally detrimental to success in our mundane undertakings." (Bogoda, 1996)

Every obstacle or temptation is an illusion that may appear in your meditation and physical life, until your "Conscious Awareness" can remain one pointed and remain in a state of "Pure Consciousness." This means you will see things clearly and not through the lens of "unconscious emotional responses" or "conditioned thinking." Some of these perceived obstacles or temptations are discussed below.

- *Obstacle or Temptation 1*: *The Senses—Sense Gratification*

The senses want pleasure now. Sex. Alcohol. A pill or drug. Food. Entertainment. These are all sense-gratifying obstacles or temptations. In meditation, they appear as thoughts. In the physical world, they appear real. Observe how you react to these thoughts in meditation. How do you react to these things in the physical world? Do you feel emotionally disturbed by these thoughts? They are just thoughts. Let them come. Let them go. Observe innocently. You must learn to control the senses, so the senses do not control you. Overindulgence in sense gratification can turn into impulsive obsessions or bad habits based on a lack of knowledge. You are not your senses. Humans have senses as part of a survival mechanism; however, in today's world, many issues arise because we abuse our senses because we do not yet know the potential power we possess (Bogoda, 1996).

- *Obstacle or Temptation 2*: *Hatred—Ill Will*

Anger and hatred will only breed more anger and hatred. Allow your Self to let go of what you like and dislike. Try to develop a more compassionate unconditional love. Try to see everyone as if they are a little child who is trying to learn; sometimes, you may even need to see yourself as a little child. Treat your Self with love and compassion. If others have ill will or act hatefully, it is probably coming from the pain or negative experiences they have suffered or from a lack of knowledge. Treat them with kindness. Have compassion for those who cannot help themselves (Bogoda, 1996).

- *Obstacle or Temptation 3: Laziness—Ignorance*

This is an unwillingness to learn the "Right Knowledge" because of the effort required to accept responsibility for themselves. This can arise in someone who is tired. Someone who feels defeated. Someone who has worked their entire life and is in physical pain. Someone who works every day and comes home to wild children. It only takes a small effort to direct your energy inward. But doing this will aid you in all other areas of your life (Bogoda, 1996).

- *Obstacle or Temptation 4: Anxiety—Worrying*

This is when the mind is not at peace because it is stuck on memories of the past or imaginings of the future. Relax. Just let your Self be still. Close your eyes. Breathe. Meditate. Everything will be alright (Bogoda, 1996).

- *Obstacle or Temptation 5: Doubt*

Doubt is the inability to decide, the lack of resolution that prevents one from making a firm commitment to higher ideals and from pursuing the good with a steady will (Bogoda, 1996).

"These five hindrances are great handicaps to one's progress. They deprive the mind of understanding and happiness and cause much unnecessary suffering. By cultivating the five cardinal virtues — confidence, energy, mindfulness, concentration, and wisdom — and by constant effort one can reduce their harmful influence." (Bogoda, 1996)

- *How Do We Remove These Obstacles or Temptations?*

The solution to these obstacles is to observe your "Conscious Awareness." As you continue to practice meditation and live in the physical world, you will encounter all types of obstacles and temptations even more than those above. However, all obstacles or temptations are illusions until you can remain one pointed on your "Conscious Awareness" or "Pure Consciousness."

I suggest you try to live from there. Live from a place of "Conscious Awareness." This will help you to navigate through life more effectively as you will not be distracted by things that hinder your growth and development. Some of the things that block many people these days are in their subconscious—things they are not even aware of.

It has been a process of becoming more aware of my own self and the issues I've faced that have given me the clarity to understand how other people are functioning and why. This clarity is yours to be had but it takes a little effort and energy. You have to take the steps. I can only point the way and suggest what I believe will help you based on what helped me and on what my intuition believes will help you. It is you that needs to walk the path.

I am here to provide guidance. Just keep reading. Keep breathing. Keep meditating.

Desire, Action, and Impression

What is desire? Desire is the feeling of "wanting something."

What is an example of desire? Why am I here? To write this. Why are you here? To read this. Are we seeking something? Are we bored? Are we lonely? Knowledge? Happiness? Love? What is it that we want? Do our desires differ? What is it that makes us individuals? What is it that makes us similar?

If you are hungry, you probably want food.

When the basic human needs, safety, air, water, food, shelter, are met, we usually desire something else or something more, do we not? Once we get something to eat, we then want to do something? Do we desire to be educated or entertained? Do we desire excitement and adventure? Do we desire love, success, money, happiness?

That desire creates an impulse for us to act in order to try and fulfill our desires. The fulfillment or attempt to fulfill our desire creates an impression that influences our perception. That impression remains with us and becomes part of our perception and then leads to another desire.

Does our happiness depend on our ability to fulfill our desires?

If we desire a certain body image and we achieve it, will that create lasting happiness, or will we then want something more—bigger muscles, less body fat, tanner, tighter skin? If we are unable to achieve the body image we desire, will it be detrimental to our self-esteem and create the illusion and impression of feeling incapable or unworthy. We are more than just our bodies.

If we desire a companion, and cannot find one, will we feel lonely? What if we do find a companion and their desire is to have children? Can you see how this cycle continues no matter what desire you have and no matter what action you take, an impression will be left? Action and Consequence. Cause and Effect.

Where do our desires come from? Some desires come from primal human instinct. Some come from our own person or individuality. Some can be imposed on us by our family, friends, coworkers, educational system, governments, and other structures of society. In our current society, the general tendency is to go to college, get a job, get married and raise a family, and so on. This cycle of desire, action, and impression continues and can leave us feeling unfulfilled or stressed by the never-ending pursuit of our own desires. What's the solution?

Contentment

How do we free ourselves from this cycle of desire, action, and impression? Contentment.

The one who seeks contentment will not find it. The one who Is, does.

-DUSTIN MATTHEWS (TO BE DETERMINED)

Contentment is a state of Being. Freedom from the cycle of desire, action, and impression. This state of "Being" brings contentment. This can be cultivated through the practice of meditation.

It is the experience of "being at peace." This can happen first during meditation and can be cultivated so that it lasts even outside of meditation in activity. As I was writing this portion of the book, I began to experience contentment and didn't feel the need to write anything more.

Worldly Affairs

Ah, yes, the material world. The "real world" as the masses call it. This is actually not the "real world" at all. But we have to act as if this material world exists and matters to uphold order and structure.

Humans need their primary needs to be met in order to survive— shelter, air, water, food. Once these basic needs are met, humans will seek something more whether consciously or subconsciously. Self-realization. However, the world seems to be going in a direction that promotes excessive material gain leaving less time and energy to focus on Self-realization or spiritual knowledge.

Some people said that I needed to return to reality because my imagination was out of touch with reality. In "reality," they didn't understand the Laws of Nature and "Pure Potentiality" and how with enough "brain power" or "coherence" or "faith," I could manifest my visions into "reality." And I still do. But I've now learned how not to be swayed by the opinions of others. Peer pressure. Conforming to society. That's just not for me. I've got a vision and that's what I'm pursuing.

But as I evolved, my desires changed. At first, it was fun to manifest becoming a better athlete, making love to beautiful women, recording a rap album, doing comedy, but along the way, my heart began to purify, and my desires changed.

What is worth desiring here in the physical world? It's alright to desire making money and having a spouse and children if that's what you want. It is important to have enough money to take care of your Self and your family and try to help others. But then what?

Developing a state of "Being" and feeling "content" does not mean giving up on life in the "material world." "Being content" does not mean you won't be successful in the "material world." "Being content" means you are not dependent on outside circumstances to make you happy. It means that no matter what is happening in the "material world" around you, you are stable and complete in your Self. It means you have harnessed your senses and are an unwavering beacon of light in times of darkness. Knowledge in times of ignorance. Hope in times of despair.

So, the best way not to be ruled by the "material world" and "desire" is to practice meditation; through this practice you will grow to "be content," which will free you from "desire." Next stop ... enlightenment.

And if you choose to record a rap album, write a self-help book, and do comedy videos, which are supported by the Laws of Nature, maybe you will make some money as a byproduct. Remember the Law of Cause and Effect.

You have a right to perform your prescribed duties, but you are not entitled to the fruits of your actions. Never consider yourself to be the cause of the results of your activities, nor be attached to inaction.

-BHAGAVAD GITA, CH. 2.V. 47

It is also important to understand that you need to play the hand you're dealt.

What does that mean?

Every individual is born into different circumstances, with varying karma and life lessons that need to be learned. Where were you born? What country? How is the culture and economy there? Do you wake up sleeping on the ground in a grass hut with eight other people and have to walk ten miles just to get clean water, or do you wake up in your own bed with a bathroom down the hall where you can drink from the faucet and then take a shower? Does your family have the wealth to send you to a private school, or did you have to sacrifice pursuing an education as a child to work and help support your family?

Many people, many circumstances. Lessons. Be grateful for what you have. Accept where you are and learn what you need to learn. Help others. I believe the reason so many people in the Western World are addicted to things such as food, drugs, alcohol, sex, and materialism is the result of how we were raised. Our basic needs are met, but we overconsume in an attempt to fill a void that can only be filled by more transcendental/spiritual means. Do we seek something outside ourselves to fulfill the emptiness we feel? How many people out there have everything they need in the physical world and crave something more? How many people realize they seek Self-realization? Not all people have reached this point. It is a point of growth and evolution. Many don't even understand what it is they are seeking or experiencing. Evolution of consciousness. Spiritual growth. We're All Connected.

Some struggle just to survive the day. They wake up and work, day after day, year after year, just to be able to provide enough money to shelter, clothe, feed, and educate their families and loved ones. But how many are overweight, addicted to drugs, alcohol, food, sex, and so on? Why didn't our educational systems provide a better understanding of the world when we were children? Why didn't our educational system teach us healthy ways to deal with stress and how to overcome our emotional issues? Why have we been educated based on a standard curriculum? Why have we been conditioned to fit in a box and conform to regularity? How much responsibility should the government take for education? Why isn't meditation taught in schools?

In my experience, a psychological/spiritual understanding of reality provided much more than any other objective knowledge. I believe that meditation is fundamental for human development. However, in my experience the general educational system today is missing something that should be fundamental.

With the volume and diversity of students in the general education setting today, it's a hard task for the general education system to cater to the needs of each individual. This is the reason for general classes and standardized testing in language, math, science, history, health/physical education and the arts. In my opinion, consciousness-based education would be a more holistic approach to education, which will benefit each individual and the collective as a whole by incorporating the practice of meditation. Fortunately, there is already a program that delivers certified teachers of Transcendental Meditation to work in schools and teach students. For more information look up, the David Lynch Foundation and the Quiet Time Program at www.davidlynchfoundation.org.

What Is Consciousness-Based Education?

Consciousness-based education is a more holistic approach to educating individuals from the inside out. An analogy would be that a student is a like a cup and objective knowledge is like the liquid going into the cup. If the cup is broken or has a leak, it will not be able to retain all of the liquid. With the practice of Transcendental Meditation, the individual can increase their own ability to learn and actually begin to heal themselves of any leaks (emotional, mental, and physical stresses) and even expand the size of their cup or increase their own capacity to learn.

Instead of placing so much focus on cramming objective knowledge into students, as the general education curriculum does, consciousness-based education incorporates the Transcendental Meditation program and allows students to explore their own subjective development from the inside. This is a way to help students integrate the objective knowledge as well as all of the other experiences they are having in this life.

What Else Could It Include?

Consciousness-based education could also include morning yoga consisting of asanas, sun salutations, pranayama, and group meditations. From there, students would enjoy a lesson by a health or nutritional teacher or chef before mealtimes on the daily selection of organic vegetarian meals they have prepared. This would increase the student's awareness to make more healthy conscious decisions with respect to what they put into their bodies. It could also incorporate physical education, health education as well as music and the arts into the schools with more appropriate funding.

Example of Consciousness Based-Education Daily Schedule (K–12)

If we, as educators, lead by example and place more priority on the health and holistic human development of our students, it will pay off exponentially in the development of the individual over time. This, in turn, will increase the holistic development of the collective society.

- 7:30 a.m. Meet in gymnasium or homeroom for attendance

- 7:35 a.m. Asanas, sun salutations, breathing techniques (pranayama), Transcendental Meditation

- 8:20 a.m. Lesson on breakfast choices on projection screen to each class or in the cafeteria

- 8:25 a.m. Breakfast

- 8:50 a.m. Classes for the next three hours to include one five- to ten-minute break for every forty-five-minute class (scientifically, there should be a small break in activity every eighteen minutes)

- 11:50 a.m. Lesson on lunch choices on projection screen to each class or in the cafeteria

- 12:00 p.m. Lunch

- 12:30 p.m. Afternoon classes should also include one five- to ten-minute break for every forty-five-minute class (scientifically, there should be a small break in activity every eighteen minutes)

- 2:00 p.m. Meet in gymnasium/auditorium or homeroom for Transcendental Meditation

- 3:00 p.m. After-school extracurricular activities: sports, music, drama …

This example was created to show the potential of a more holistic style of consciousness-based education while still including enough time for general education classes necessary for students to learn and develop. This schedule includes enough class time for six forty-five-minute classes per day or a block schedule of three ninety-minute classes per day.

From my teaching experience, there are some classes that students would benefit from in shorter lengths and longer lengths. For example, physical education, health education, and English classes would be better to have daily in shorter durations to ensure students are practicing a healthy amount each day. But if there is a science experiment that includes lab time, it might be more beneficial to have the block schedule. Or even a combo of both. M-W six 45-minute classes. Th-F three 90-minute classes.

There is also some emerging research in support of starting high school later in the morning because teenagers need more sleep for better brain development. If starting school later for high schoolers were to happen, I would suggest a 9 am start and using a similar schedule as the one above, adjusting the times accordingly.

Acceptance and Forgiveness

In order to grow, we must learn to accept that the past is in the past and the only thing we can do is learn from it. Forgive your Self and others for what happened in the past and accept that you will need to be forgiving throughout this process. Forgiveness is for you. When you forgive someone for something they have done to you, it makes you feel better. Let it go. Sometimes we will seek forgiveness from others but what we really need to do is forgive ourselves.

Stop looking for fault in things/people/circumstances to blame. Accept what Is. Accept life as an ongoing opportunity to learn, a challenge, a dream; it is what we make it. Accepting this and learning to forgive yourself and others is hard to do especially when you are in pain and suffering. Try to be a student of life, not a victim of circumstance.

To overcome pain and suffering, sometimes you have to go through the five stages of grief which include: denial, anger, bargaining, depression, and acceptance. When you finally accept the loss of a loved one or the feelings of a broken heart, it is transcending. It will feel like a weight has been lifted off of your shoulders. Leave the past behind, you have a bright future ahead. But realize, too, that your future is constantly being created by the decisions you make in the present moment.

You have the freewill to choose your own fate. Forgive yourself and accept that everyone has made mistakes but own up to them and progress onward with your life. Realign your thoughts, feelings, and behaviors so you can live a better life in harmony with the Laws of Nature.

Accept that you can't change the past. You can only learn from it. So, forgive the old person you used to be and be a better version of your Self today. The only way to continue positive growth is to forgive yourself so you can focus completely on making your Self better in the present.

This can be difficult. The way I found the strength to forgive my Self for not answering the phone when my best friend called a week before he over-dosed and passed away, the way I have overcome feelings of betrayal from past lovers and close friends, the way I forgave myself for being addicted to alcohol and drugs for so many years, the way I forgave and accepted what I perceived to be a subpar collegiate football career, was with meditation, prayer, surrender and some other things listed in this book. It all comes down to gaining and applying the "right knowledge". You can do it.

Love

I'm pretty sure all humans have the desire to love and be loved.
-DUSTIN MATTHEWS (TO BE DETERMINED)

Love is the most powerful of all emotions. I consider emotion to be energy in motion. So really, emotion is how we *feel* energy. Love is essential in the process of self-discovery. Most importantly—for your Self.

You need to learn how to love your Self before you can properly love someone else. This requires compassion, acceptance, forgiveness, and trust. Trust that love will guide you.

Also be careful not to confuse love with lust. Love is heartfelt while lust is more primal. In other words, lust is in the flesh, love is in the eyes.

Unconditional love is what we should all strive to be and give. In order to love unconditionally it means being able to accept and forgive your Self and others. It means communicating the truth openly and honestly with compassion. It means listening with a compassionate heart and trying to understand the perspective of others from a non-judgmental point of view.

It takes more strength to open your heart than it does to close it. If your heart is closed, it cannot give or receive the love, it so desires. If your heart has been broken, I can empathize with you. But it's important to understand it was only broken to be made stronger. In the moment, it may not seem that way but have faith and in time you will start to understand.

By applying the knowledge in *IMAGINE: The Simple Steps to Success,* you can heal a broken heart if that is your goal. I've healed my heart, mind, body, and soul over and over, all by gaining and devoting my life to applying the "right knowledge." It takes effort and energy. But you can do it. Just start taking these steps. One step at a time. You will start to see.

Love is patient. Love is kind. Love is waiting; give it time.
-DUSTIN MATTHEWS (TO BE DETERMINED)

Why do I feel so driven by the love in my own heart? How are you supposed to tell someone how you feel everything? When you meet them. You'll know. It will feel strange. Mysterious. Is there really chemistry between people? Compatible energies? What is it that draws us to certain people?

Hey, whoa! Take it easy, Romeo!

Faith

Throughout this process, there might be hard times and you may want to quit or think this book isn't working. My question to you is: Why do you think it is the book that is not working and not yourself? Are you resisting the necessary changes that might have to be made in order to really change your life? Why? Fear not. And please, trust that what I'm telling you will help you, if you learn how to help your Self. Patience.

There might be days when you feel like giving up. Days when you don't want to get out of bed. Days when you feel like you don't want to be alive. Days when you question your relationships. Days when you contemplate your reason for being here on this planet. But it will be faith that will get you through those days. Have faith that those days won't last forever. And keep meditating. You will start to pick your Self up.

There are still days when I get down and feel like things are not going the way I want them to, but then I'm reminded by the faith in my heart and mind and know that I'm right where I need to be. So, I needed to write this part in the book today, but it needed to experience before it was understood. Many lessons in life are repeated until you understand them and make the necessary changes to live a better life. What lessons do you think you need to learn?

There will be trials and tribulations along your path in life. You may suffer injuries, heartbreaks, uncertainty, loss of loved ones, guilt, shame, depression, addiction, sickness, and disease. You may feel like you've made a lot of bad decisions and you can never redeem your Self. But you can. Learn from your experiences and believe you can change. I did. You can too.

Sometimes faith is earned in the darkest of times. Sometimes, your struggles are necessary to make you stronger. Understand that there is something more powerful that you may not be able to comprehend in your times of strife. But have faith that you will make it through. Prayer can be a great way to instill you with the faith you need to make it through difficult times. Over time you will see how your faith is what has kept you going all along. Your experiences will strengthen your Faith and someday you will see. Keep the faith, my friend.

"Thank you, God, for filling my heart and mind with all of your faith and strength. Thank you, God, for removing all doubt and fear from my heart and mind and letting only faith and strength remain. Thank you, God, for filling me with all of your faith."

I am healthy. I am strong. I am worthy. I am willing. I am ready. I am able.

Prayers

It can be hard to forgive someone you think has hurt you or wronged you in some way. I have found that praying along with meditation helps free me from negative energy or emotions. The following paragraph provides advice on what I think prayers are and how I practice my prayers.

The spoken word is very powerful. Especially with the intention of that prayer being heard and answered by God/the Universe in whatever way that is best regarding your situation. I refer to God as He because that's who God is to me. But I think in reality, God is beyond gender. But from my experience, God does hear our prayers and does answer them.

You may feel God as a small voice in your head or as the feeling of a weight being lifted in times of strife. You may receive a loving text message or hear a song on the radio at just the right moment. I've had many validating experiences, but one of my favorites was in a lucid dream at a time in my life when I doubted God's existence. In my dream, I asked in my head if God was real and was immediately awoken by the loudest crack of thunder I've ever heard. It was pretty convincing. Keep your mind and heart open to receive these messages. The Lord works in mysterious ways. He might even be trying to talk to you right now.

I've learned that using gratitude in prayers adds magnitude to them and makes them more powerful. I've developed my own way of praying over the years. I used to pray before all my football and baseball games. Even though I don't really go to church and people may not view me as religious, I've prayed just about every day since I was seventeen years old, when my father recited *The Lord's Prayer* to me.

Our Father who art in Heaven, hallowed be thy name.

Thy Kingdom come, thy will be done, on Earth as it is in Heaven.

Give us this day our daily bread and forgive us our trespasses as we forgive those who trespass against us.

And lead us not into temptation but deliver us from evil.

For thine is the Kingdom, the Power and the Glory, Forever and ever.

Amen.

I've developed my own personal relationship with God over time, and it just keeps getting better. I usually maintain a pretty open dialogue with God all day, and some people may think I'm crazy, talking to my Self out loud, but I just laugh because if I said I'm talking to God they would think I'm even crazier. I love it.

In a lot of my darkest hours, I'd be overwhelmed with sadness or rage and it was difficult to believe praying would do anything. But after surviving, I realized those experiences only strengthened my faith in God. I prayed through all of my pain and suffering. I prayed through all the tears and gasping for air to breathe. I prayed for God to kill me and take me away from all my suffering. I've been there. I've wanted to die. It was awful then, but now I see it was beautiful!

By the grace of God, I'm still here and I'm stronger in spirit or higher in my development of consciousness. I've surrendered my life to God and now I strive to do God's will, not mine. Because God's will is mine. God knows what is best for me and I trust God to lead me on the right path in life.

Now when I pray, I usually go with what I feel in my heart in that moment. Most nights, I will sit on my bed and meditate for a few minutes to calm my Self, and then, I begin speaking out loud or softly in my own mind. I start with whatever is most full in my heart.

I often repeat my prayers until I really *feel* them. I start by emptying all of the negative energy and then filling myself with positive energy.

The prayers I use are based on what I feel in my heart. You can try and see how it feels for you. I often feel like exhaling rather forcefully if my heart is heavy with emotion. If I'm really feeling sad and hurting, I'll even shake out my arms as if I were shaking loose the negative emotions.

Allow your intuition to guide you. Do what you feel your heart desires. It's okay to cry and breathe deeply. It's okay to scream into your pillow. Sometimes, heavy stress needs to be released in a way that most humans are ashamed of discussing. But it's alright. Let it out. Let it go.

Once you've released the negative emotions or thoughts through gratitude or de-stressing through deep breathing, crying, or a physical movement, allow your Self to continue praying. Oftentimes, you may feel tired from releasing heavy emotions and need to sleep or rest that's perfectly fine. Sometimes you may question if it's working because you are so focused on that negative emotion. But as my therapist and acting coach have told me, "The way out, is through."

So feel it. Let it come. Let it go. Naturally. You can't force a cut to heal, it takes time. But you can address the wound. Same for emotions. You can't force a broken heart to heal. But you can take some steps to help heal over time.

The point of the gratitude prayer is to redirect your focus in a positive way, so that you change your perception. If you stay focused on the negative, you stay in the cycle of suffering and reliving painful memories or experiences. This can be called *wallowing*. But when you switch your focus to something positive, it will get you out of that old rut or that old way of thinking.

Some people call this *mood making* or *emotionalism*, but I think it is important to fully experience the emotion and then let it go. If a feeling is there, then feel it and release it. Resisting it or holding onto it just causes more pain and suffering. I've been working on this for years and it does take time. But it gets easier with practice.

So, keep practicing. You can practice this anytime and anywhere. You don't have to be at church or alone in your bedroom to pray. I often pray when I feel a negative thought or emotion surfacing. When I feel it come up as a little thought bubble. If it's negative, I pop it. How? I use my gratitude guns (*Gratitude Prayers*).

Try it for your Self. Prayer and self-talk are very similar. And using gratitude, which is a grateful attitude, provides the best results. Do it until it works. It will strengthen over time. You just have to imagine your Self getting stronger each time you do it. It's like a video game and you're leveling up the more you do it.

My faith is like a muscle and I work out every day!

-DUSTIN MATTHEWS (TO BE DETERMINED)

The following page is a list of prayers that I have used in the past and still continue to use. I usually start with, "Thank you, God." But you can use what feels most fitting for you.

Thank you, God, for freeing me from all negative thoughts and emotions.

Thank you, God, for freeing me from all pain and suffering.

Thank you, God, freeing me from all anger and jealousy.

Thank you, God, for freeing me from all fear and doubt.

Thank you, God, for freeing me from all greed and envy.

Thank you, God, for freeing me from all worry and anxiety.

Thank you, God, for freeing me from all self-judgment and unworthiness.

Thank you, God, for freeing me from all guilt and shame.

Thank you, God, for freeing me from all blame and sin.

Thank you, God, for freeing me from all hate and evil.

Thank you, God, for freeing me from any unhealthy emotional attachments.

Thank you, God, for helping me forgive myself and anyone I feel has hurt me.

Thank you, God, for blessing me with all of your grace and fullness.

Thank you, God, for blessing me with all of your love and compassion.

Thank you, God, for blessing me with all of your strength and courage.

Thank you, God, for blessing me with all of your faith and hope.

Thank you, God, for blessing me with all of your knowledge and wisdom.

Thank you, God, for blessing me with all of your peace and serenity.

Thank you, God, for blessing me with all of your health and happiness.

Thank you, God, for blessing me with all of your prosperity and abundance.

Thank you, God, for blessing me with all of your joy and passion.

Thank you, God, for blessing me with all of your creativity and confidence.

Chanting

I've come to understand chanting as a form of prayer, which is repeated to resonate at a certain frequency and cause a desired effect. Chanting in the Vedic tradition is usually done in Sanskrit or Devanagari, which is considered to be the "Language of Nature." I was fortunate to learn a small part of this language at Maharishi International University when I was working on my degree in Vedic Science.

Research has found that Transcendental Meditation and Vedic Chanting have positive effects on individual and collective brain function. Some believe chanting should be listened to by Vedic Pandits who are basically the priests of the Vedic Tradition. But sometimes, I like to do my own chanting. It feels more personal and I like feeling the vibrations resonate from within my chest not just my mind. I've also recorded some of my favorite chants. Many chants are simple mantras that are repeated 108 times. In the Vedic tradition, 108 is a sacred number used when reciting chants.

Some of the chants I practice are based on my Jyotish, or Vedic astrology, which I will discuss in a moment. But first, the following is a list of the chants that I practice and/or listen to as recordings. To access my personal archive of recorded chants go to:

www.dustinmatthewsmedia.com

Aum Namaha Shivaya

Aum Hreem Kleem Namaha

Aum Han Hanumate Namaha

Aum Gan Ganapataye Namaha

Aum Shri Mahalakshmi Namaha

I was initiated into the practice of Transcendental Meditation, which I suggest doing before any chanting. I think Transcendental Meditation is more powerful than chanting, but both are beneficial. Devotion to the practice will grow as you continue to practice it. Try to be aware of how you feel when you let go of your expectations and just focus on performing the action or just listening without expectations.

STEP 3:
GET A VEDIC ASTROLOGY (JYOTISH) READING AND TAKE A PERSONALITY TEST

Vedic Astrology (Jyotish) and a Personality Test

Vedic astrology, also known as Jyotish, is a mathematical calculation of the alignment of the planets at a specific moment in time. This study is done based on the time and place an individual was born. The locations of the planets at the time of birth will have an influence on that individual throughout their life.

This type of ancient knowledge has been studied for many thousands of years and can allow one to see the trends and tendencies of an individual in their lifetime. This knowledge can be of great assistance to those seeking a better understanding of themselves or to those who wish to find their true calling in life. A Jyotish reading provides individuals with more clarity and insight to make better career decisions, relationship decisions, financial decisions, and so on. This knowledge is available for individuals to try and find their ideal path and live a healthier, happier, more peaceful, and prosperous life.

Below is an image of my personal Vedic Astrology (Jyotish) Birth Chart. The letters represent the planets, and the twelve houses each represent one of the twelve zodiac signs. Each of these signs and houses represent different things and have varying influences on many aspects of life. After learning the practice of Transcendental Meditation, I suggest getting a Vedic Astrology (Jyotish) reading as Step 3. It will help you align with your dharma or destiny, which has been written in the stars and is of course up to you to discover. There are a lot of different websites where you can get free Vedic Astrology (Jyotish) readings; the site I like is: www.indastro.com.

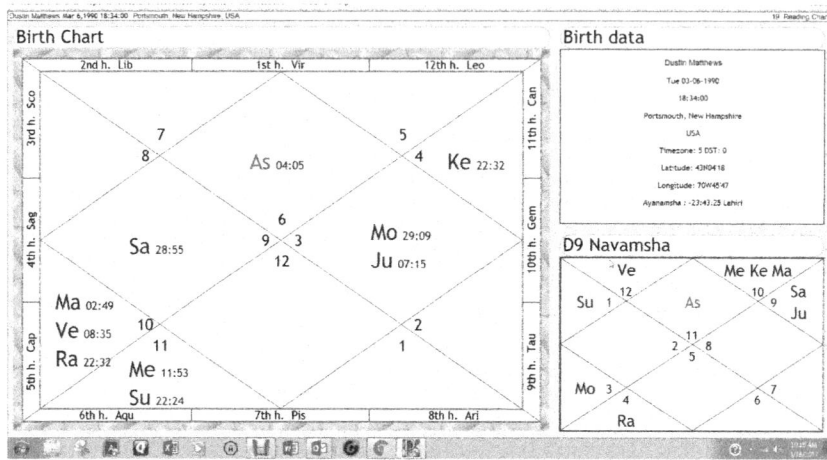

Another way to attain more clarity and direction is to take a personality test. The Myers Briggs Type Indicator is a really cool personality test, which can provide insight into figuring out your own individual personality. I recommend taking the free test at www.16personalities.com.

They have an abundance of information about which personality type you are and how you might be best suited for certain types of career paths. It isn't set in stone but it does provide some great insight based on our psychology. I think it's important to get an idea of who we are at a deeper level if we want to be truly satisfied.

Gemstones and Herbs

Everything in this Universe is, at its most fundamental level, considered energy. Yes, even gemstones and herbs possess a vibrational frequency, which can affect other energies and even work synergistically with one another.

When an individual holds or wears gemstones or consumes herbal supplements, they may feel a subtle change in their energy or mood depending on their level of sensitivity. Some may feel nothing.

Caffeine, for example, can come from coffee beans or tea leaves. Caffeine is used primarily for the stimulating effects it has on the central nervous system. Most pharmaceutical drugs today have been manipulated or chemically extracted, synthesized, or enhanced from plants and herbs. There are natural remedies that the Earth has provided in the form of gemstones and herbs that are available for us to discover and utilize.

One herb that has some medicinal benefits and may be a better alternative than pharmaceuticals is marijuana. My experiences with marijuana have varied. Regardless of today's perspectives around this plant, I've learned a lot from my experiences with marijuana. In times of addiction, it showed me a way out. In times of depression, it showed me happiness. In times of self-pity, it showed me what I had to be grateful for.

Marijuana can somehow act as medicine for the soul, providing us with what we need whether we know it or not. I've also heard marijuana be called the *lazy man's meditation*. As with all things in life, moderation and balance seem to work best. This isn't a permission slip to use and abuse drugs. I no longer use marijuana to get high. I feel the high that one really wants to keep is a state of contentment, and I've found that meditation is a gentler, more sustainable technique to accomplish the things I desire.

Ayurveda in the Vedic tradition is defined as the "Knowledge of Life." It is the study of natural or holistic health, which brings balance to the mind and body. One of the most popular remedies that go hand in hand with Ayurveda is meditation. However, there is much more we can learn from the study of Ayurveda, such as the effects of different foods, herbs, and spices.

There is also much to learn about the metaphysical properties of gemstones. Metaphysical properties are like the attributes of a certain gemstone or metal. There are many different gemstones and metals with varying metaphysical properties. There is a reason for the prices of precious gems and metals such as gold and silver being so high. They were valued in ancient times for their metaphysical properties or "magical powers" that people felt when they came in contact with them. And even still today, that magical energy is alive.

Is There a Difference between Metaphysical Properties and Magical Powers?

I believe both of these phrases attempt to describe the same phenomenon. Can the subtle energy of wearing a gemstone have an effect on an individual? What if that individual cannot feel it? Is it not there? What if there is no scientifically valid evidence of something? Does that mean it is not real or have we just not discovered a means to measure it yet?

You cannot see the wind or the air. Yet you feel the breeze on your skin and the breath in your lungs. You cannot see the fragrance of a flower, but you can smell it in the air.

Fear not what you don't know.

Keep learning.

Habits

Habit: A settled or regular tendency or practice, especially one that is hard to give up.

Watch your thoughts, they become words; watch your words, they become actions; watch your actions, they become habits; watch your habits, they become character; watch your character, for it becomes your destiny.

-LAO TZU

How to Break a Habit?

*"95% of what we think, feel, do, or achieve is the result
of a learned habit."*

(DARREN HARDY, *THE COMPOUND EFFECT*, 2010)

First, take some time for self-reflection (meditation) and life inventory. By expanding your conscious awareness, you can begin to identify what habits are beneficial and which habits you want to break. Are they habitual thought patterns or habitual patterns of behavior (subtle level or gross level)?

"No problem can be solved from the same level of consciousness that created it."

-ALBERT EINSTEIN

Habits = Routine - Cue - Reward

As we continuously engage in certain patterns of thought or behavior, it has an effect on our brains. The effect is like traveling on a dirt road over and over again until the ruts in the road are deeper and deeper, making it harder to get out of those old ruts. But that road goes to the same place over and over again. If we want to create new brain connections, we need to break free from those habitual ruts that we've been stuck in. I've found that the simplest way to break a habit on the grossest level of relativity is to introduce a new "cue" to replace the old behavior.

For example: Instead of hanging out with friends and playing video games after school, replace that behavior with going to the gym and engaging in some physical activity. Replace the old behavior (playing video games) with a new behavior (exercise, writing, learning to play an instrument, etc.). These are just a few examples of how you can use a substitute for that habitual behavior that you don't want to do.

To break habits on a more subtle level, meditation or therapy is more effective.

What you put your attention on grows strong in your life.

-MAHARISHI

Develop "Good" Habits or a "Good" Routine

What is a habit? Why does "good" have quotation marks? A habit is something you do repeatedly. "Good" is a word that I am using as a synonym for "healthy" or "life supporting."

What are some bad habits? Smoking, drinking, gambling, drug abuse, sex abuse, overeating, binge-watching Netflix, laziness, and so on. Yeah, I know; I've been there.

What are some "good" habits that can increase your overall level of health and well-being? Meditation, yoga, organic vegetarian diet, drinking more water, reading, writing, art, music, exercising, and so on.

How do we change bad habits into good habits? Substitute them. What is your daily routine like now? Use the time management sheet, which is coming up in a few pages, to document your life in real time. Identify what changes you can make and start implementing them now.

Do you start your day with a few cups of coffee and a few cigarettes? Try waking up in the morning and doing yoga and meditating before you start drinking coffee. See if it helps. See if you notice your stress and anxiety levels being released during your yoga and meditation, so you don't feel the need for as much, if any, caffeine or nicotine.

Let's say you watch four hours of television every night before bed and then you can't fall asleep. Instead, start reading or writing or doing something creative before bed. It may seem different or difficult at first but observe yourself as you're doing it.

So, let's say you go out and socialize and drink with friends and make decisions you regret like drinking too much, using drugs, or being promiscuous and hooking up with strangers. Again, try something new. Go to the gym and work out, take a yoga class, take a cooking class, learn to meditate, develop a creative hobby.

It is just a matter of redirecting your effort and energy. You can do it.

The Horse of Your Habits and the Boy and the Tree

Here, there are a couple of analogies to consider.

The first one takes place in the late 1500s when people still rode horses on dirt roads and lived in castles. Imagine the *Game of Thrones* era. So, each morning before anyone else woke up, a working-class peasant walked along the dirt road toward the castle with his wagon of goods to set up in the best location just inside the castle gate. Every morning on the peasant's way to the castle, a knight on a beautiful black horse exited the castle gates and galloped by at full speed, riding toward the outer villages. Each day, the peasant wondered where the knight was off to in such a hurry. After a few days, the peasant decided to ask the knight where he was going.

So, one morning as the knight came sprinting by on his horse, the peasant yelled to him, "Where are you going?" And the knight responded, "I don't know, ask the horse." This analogy portrays your habits being the controlling influence in your life. And if you don't take control of them, they will take control of you.

The next story is about a boy and the tree. One day, a wise man and boy were walking through a forest. The wise man said to the boy, "Today, I will teach you about the power of your habits." The boy was only about seven years old, but he was excited to learn. As they walked, the wise man came to a stop and, pointing to a small sapling about 6 inches high, said to the boy, "Boy, pull up that sprout of a sapling." The boy went over to the small sprout of a sapling and pulled it out of the ground with casc. "That was easy." The boy replied.

They continued to walk down the trail. "Boy pull up that sapling," the wise man said again, pointing to a sapling that was about knee high. The boy ran over to the sapling and pulled it out with a little effort.

They walk a little further. "Boy, pull up that sapling," the wise man said again, pointing to a sapling that was as tall as the boy. The boy ran over and shook the tree and struggled for about a minute but eventually pulled up the sapling and its roots.

"I got it," the boy said, now with some sweat on his brow as he wiped his forehead.

They walked a little further and the wise man pointed to a very tall and strong-looking oak tree, too big for even a grown man to wrap his arms around. "Boy, pull up that tree."

The boy stopped and said, "I'm sorry, but I don't think I can pull up that tree."

The wise man said, "My boy, you have just learned a powerful lesson on the power that habits can have in your life. Habits are like these trees, and the longer you let them grow in your life, the bigger they get, the deeper the roots grow, and the harder they will become to uproot. Sometimes, they can even get so big and so deeply rooted that you might not believe it's possible to uproot them" (Hardy, 2010).

Self-reflection and taking inventory of the habits and behaviors in our lives is essential to identifying our patterns of behavior. Once we recognize the patterns, we have the choice to continue taking that action or trying to change it.

What habitual behaviors are preventing you from becoming the person you want to be? Identify them. It all starts with awareness. Once you identify these behaviors, you can change them. It takes effort to reflect and look at your life objectively. But that is how you can start the process of change.

Try it out. On the chart below write down your behaviors. What behaviors align with who you want to be? What behaviors don't align with who you want to be?

Good behaviors	Bad behaviors

We Are Products of Our Environment

We are products of what we think, read, write, listen to, watch on TV, eat, drink, see, surround ourselves with, and experience. It is important to recognize how these outside stimuli can affect you. It is important to develop your mind and cultivate a state of "Conscious Awareness," which will act as your "inner guidance system" or "intuition." This will help protect you from the pollution of conditioning, mass media and negative energy.

Examples of the types of pollution by mass media and negative energy include the constant advertisement of fast food, soda, alcohol, and material goods; the abuse of sexual appeal in commercials, music videos, movies, television, pornography; the glorification and glamorization of drugs, alcohol, money and power; and the mass entertainment of violent television, movies, video games, propaganda, and so on. This list goes on and on. I'm not trying to take away people's freedom to choose what they read, eat, and watch on television, but it is important to consider how those things we "consume" affect us and others.

All these things have an impact on our minds, feelings, and behaviors individually and collectively. The overstimulation and saturation of media outlets can lead to desensitization in us as humans, which causes us to be less compassionate, empathetic, and morally stable. If people are constantly being bombarded by negative stimuli, they can start to think negative behavior is acceptable. This leads to building walls in our minds about our emotions and sensitivities about what is right and wrong.

If mass media continues to oversaturate the minds of human beings with sex, money, power, violence, hatred, evil, greed, drugs, and alcohol, the consequences will not be good. Therefore, it is important to sensor this type of stimuli and speak up about what you believe is right. As human beings, we have been desensitized, and the repercussions are apparent in the rising number of individuals suffering from health issues, obesity, drug/alcohol abuse, depression, anxiety, mass shootings and violence, and so on.

Possible solutions: Learn to meditate and take inventory into your own life. Limit or eliminate TV, video games, social media, pornography, alcohol, drugs, fast food, soda, and violence.

By doing this, you will become more aware of the impact it's had on you and others. You may notice other people acting senseless or mindless. This is a result of the mass pollution of the collective consciousness. Some of us don't even understand the haze that we live in. I've been there. Maya. Ignorance. No Bueno.

I'm not saying that if you do things like eat fast food, drink and watch violent movies or play video games that you're a bad person. All I'm saying is be careful about how much exposure you get to certain stimuli because over time it can desensitize you as a human. As a child we are more receptive and susceptible to these outside influences and need to be cautious we don't overload our systems. Like I said before this can cause trauma/desensitization or even addiction and dependency so it's important we try to reflect and regulate what it is we are taking in form our environment.

To continue with the discussion that states we are products of our environment: It is important to declutter our environment. Our surroundings have an effect on our minds. Sometimes, it's necessary to declutter and clean up our surroundings to achieve more clarity and a fresh perspective.

Make your bed in the morning. There is actually an entire book that describes the benefits and impact of the simple act of just making your bed every morning. Do it. It helps.

Clean your room. Organize your work environment or desk where you study or work. Organization can increase productivity and efficiency. Stay organized. Your environment is a reflection of you, and you are a reflection of your environment. This way, you know where your things are, and when you need them, you can easily locate them without searching all over your room and in your mind. It may take time and effort to get organized, but it will result in greater productivity later.

It will also add to your peace of mind and make you feel more successful and confident. Performing small tasks like making your bed and keeping your room clean or workspace organized has many benefits. Try it out. You'll see.

Motivation

Motivation: Motive + Activation

- Motive: A reason for doing something

- Activation: The action or process of making something active or operative

- Motivation: The reason or reasons one has for behaving in a particular way

Intrinsic Motivation: Intrinsic motivation refers to behavior that is driven by internal rewards. In other words, the motivation to engage in a behavior arises from within the individual because it is naturally satisfying to you (*self-referral*).

Extrinsic Motivation: Extrinsic motivation refers to behavior that is driven by external rewards such as money, fame, grades, and praise (*object-referral*).

How Can You Increase Intrinsic Motivation?

- Autonomy: You have a choice. Freewill.

- Competency: You are good enough to do what it is you want to do.

- Relatedness: It will have an effect on others.

Three Keys to Motivation

- *Direction*: Direction is the goal that inspires action.

- *Intensity*: Intensity is the strength of the response in that direction.

- *Persistence*: Persistence is the duration or amount of time one expends effort and energy toward their goal.

Motivation Is about Relevancy!

What is important to you?

Achieving BIG GOALS takes hard work and commitment. But it can be difficult to commit to something you don't want to do. If you don't really care about something, how can you commit to doing it? You have to LOVE it. You have to WANT it. You have to NEED it. It is borderline insanity to commit to a HUGE VISION. You need to live it and breathe it. Otherwise, it's just a dream.

Everybody has BIG DREAMS. But what separates those who achieve their dreams and those who don't is the work they put in. Not the work they put in on one day, one week, or one year. But the total accumulation of the work they put in over the course of their entire life.

Most of the time, when we look at another person's success, we only see them at their peak. We don't always see how much time, effort, and energy went into reaching that peak. We don't always see the climb or the struggle others have been through to get where they are.

The quality of the work you put into your goals plays a part as well. Are you sacrificing sleep, food, exercise, family, relationships?

Set Your Self Up for Success

How?

Decide what you want and develop a daily routine or plan of action in line with your objectives.

Recognize the BIG PICTURE. Play the LONG GAME. It won't happen overnight.

Life is a marathon not a sprint.

Burning the candle at both ends is not sustainable. It might work for a while, but it will catch up to you. Develop a sustainable routine.

You'll need better quality sleep to be more alert. You'll need better quality food to stay energized. You'll need better quality activity to stay fit. Develop habits to be more efficient at learning the skills you desire.

Prioritize

Sleep is God. Meditation is realization. Food is fuel. Exercise is efficiency. Work is will.

Decide

Although this may seem easy to some, it can be a difficult task to complete. Deciding what it is we truly want deep down can be tough. What are your true dreams and goals? If you've gotten this far, you've got an open mind. Have you learned Transcendental Meditation? Did you get your Jyotish reading? Those two things can help you find more clarity about what it is you want to do. These helped me discover what I wanted to do, which at the time was record a rap album and write this book. And then, I did it. I also played college football and became the captain of my team; because at the time that was my goal.

Once you make your decision, you will need to develop a plan of action to achieve your goals and live your dreams. If you decide you want to change your dream(s) or goal(s), that's alright, it's part of the process. You will need to self-reflect, evaluate your previous decisions, adapt, and recreate your plan of action. Self-reflection, Self-correction, Self-direction. Remember that. Self-reflection happens naturally during the process of meditation. Then you can correct and direct your Self.

STEP 4:
DECIDE WHAT YOU WANT!

Write it down. Type it up. Make it personal.

Below is my example before writing *IMAGINE: The Simple Steps to Success.*

- **Dream:** Record a rap album, write a self-help book, build a pyramid, and save the world.

- **Goal(s):** Write a book that helps people to better themselves. Teaching others how to live a better, happier more successful life is saving the world one person at a time.

- **Plan of Action:** Finish writing *IMAGINE: The Simple Steps to Success.*

  Write. Revise. Reread. Repeat. (I actually did this many, many, many times.)

  Submit to editor for review. Revise.

  Publish and market.

Experimentation

Try new things: Experiment. Experience.

An experiment is a concrete or practical method of trying something. Think of an experiment as something material like cement. Where an experience is something abstract you learn from your experiment. Science. Conscience. Presence. Conscience is made up of two words (con) meaning—with, and (science) meaning—the intellectual and practical activity encompassing the systematic study of the structure and behavior of the physical and natural world through observation and experiment.

So why is experimentation important? Experience is the best teacher. Learning through an experience is much more powerful, compelling, and convincing than other methods of learning. Subjective experiences are the most powerful experiences. What does that mean? Have you ever had an experience that convinced you of something that you didn't know was possible or real?

Having the courage to experiment and not being so afraid of failing that you don't even try is essential. I've witnessed firsthand with my Self and in others how we often construct our own mental barriers based on our conditioned thought patterns. This may come from past experiences when you tried something and someone you were close to and whose opinion you valued made fun of or judged you, which had a negative impact on you, so you gave up trying. Most often, this happens with our own parents or loved ones whose opinions we value the most.

However, you can overcome these mental barriers by engaging in those things that you're afraid of doing. Through experimentation you can break your own mental barriers and overcome your preconditioned thoughts or fears. I've witnessed athletes with a lot of physical potential, that had a mental block or lacked confidence because of previous experiences, which led them to believe they weren't good enough, and as a result they were unable to make the effort.

Finding a way to motivate these individuals for me was easy. I was convinced that they could achieve what they wanted to because I believed in them. My faith in them inspired them to continue trying and that led to positive experiences, which started building their confidence and as a result increased their effort and performance until they believed in themselves.

It all comes back to increasing the intrinsic motivation of individuals, empowering people to believe in themselves. Everyone has an unlimited potential that they can tap into with the right guidance. The sooner, the better.

What Is Your Dream? What Is Your Dharma? What Is Your Destiny?

Three words with a similar meaning. These can be explained as the purpose of your life in an exalted or dramatic way. For many, if there was no fear, no doubt, and no skepticism, it would be clear to you what it is. But it is something that can evolve. It might be your destiny today to do one thing in order to reach your destiny in the future. One step at a time, one day at a time.

Exercise: Settle your Self in meditation for a few minutes and then fill out the diagram on the next page. On the following page, there are four circles that connect in the middle. List what you love, what you're good at, what the world needs, and what the world will pay for. If there are things that fall into multiple categories, put them in the appropriate location. What is in the center circle? If there isn't enough space to write in the circles, you can write in the boxes provided below the Four-Way Venn Diagram.

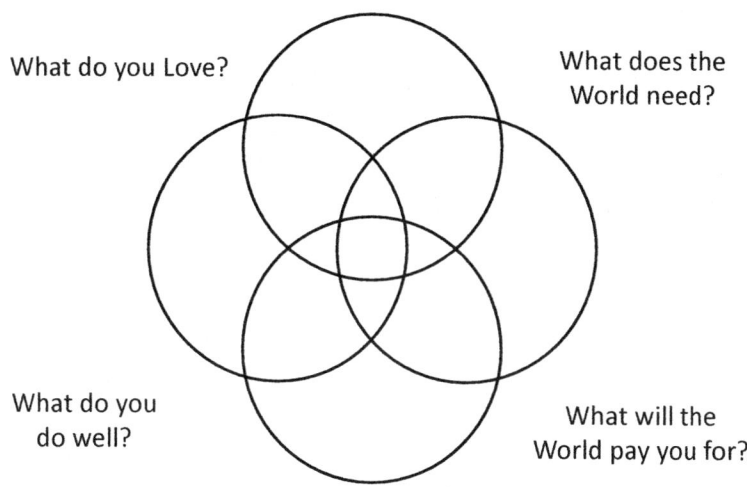

What do you Love?

What does the World need?

What do you do well?

What will the World pay you for?

What do you Love?	What does the World need?
What do you do well?	**What will the World pay you for?**

Is there something that all of these circles or boxes have in common? If so, that is most likely your Dharma or Destiny.

Goal Setting

Goal: A goal is an idea of the future or desired result that a person or a group of people envisions, plans, and commits to achieve.

No action can be performed successfully without a clear result in view.

-MAHARISHI

Expectations:

- (*Usually plural*) Looking forward to something, whether feared or hoped for.

- An attitude of expectancy or hope; anticipation.

You have a right to perform your prescribed duties, but you are not entitled to the fruits of your actions. Never consider yourself to be the cause of the results of your activities, nor be attached to inaction.

-BHAGAVAD GITA CH.2 V.47

Translation: Perform action for the sake of the action. Performing actions for results can cause emotional distress when the expected results are not met, which can impede growth.

Insanity is repeating the same behavior and expecting a different result.

-ALBERT EINSTEIN

Goal setting is experimental. There will be challenges. Be flexible and learn from mistakes.

Find Your Flow

As you begin to challenge yourself and move away from your comfort zone, it's important to ensure that your current skill level can meet the level of challenge. Too hard of a challenge can create anxiety or fear of failure. Too easy of a challenge can cause boredom. As you continue to hone your skills, you need to raise the bar on the level of challenge you create for yourself. Try to get out of your comfort zone and into your challenge zone but not into the panic zone.

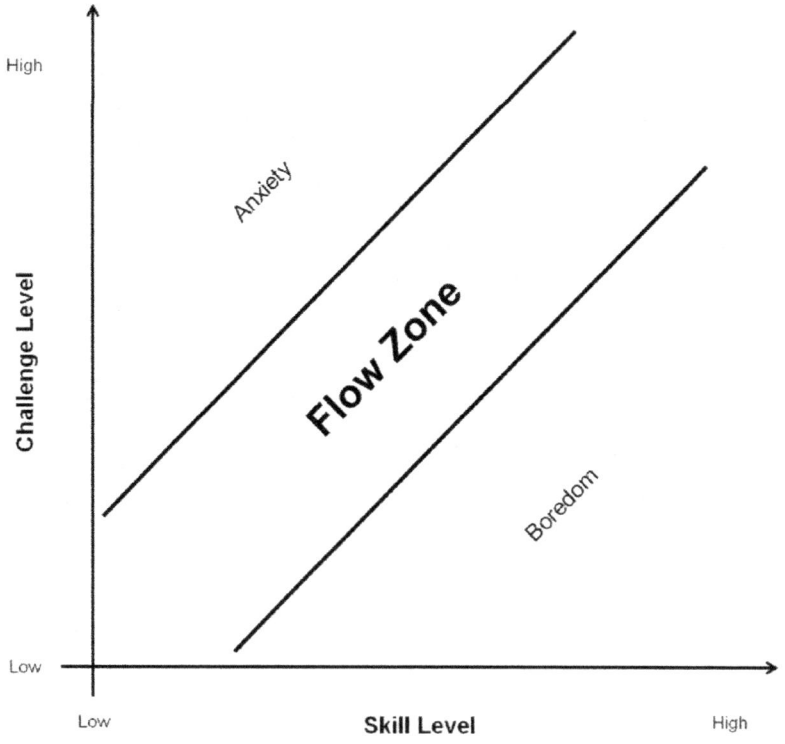

Note. Adapted from Csikszentmihalyi, Mihaly (1990). *Flow: The Psychology of Optimal Experience*. Harper & Row: New York, NY.

SMART Goals

SMART is an acronym for a framework of the important elements to consider with goal setting.

- **Specific**—What exactly do you want to achieve? Be specific and detailed.

- **Measurable**—Is the goal measurable? Objective goals are more concrete or quantitative.

- **Attainable**—Is your goal attainable for you? Do you have the skills/resources/energy?

- **Relevant**—Is your goal important to you?

- **Timely**—Do you have a deadline for your goal?

Note. Adapted from Scott, S.J. (2014) *S.M.A.R.T. Goals Made Simple.* Archangel Ink.

SMART Goals

Statement:	
Specific?	
Measurable?	
Attainable?	
Relevant?	
Timely?	

Note. Adapted from Scott, S.J. (2014) *S.M.A.R.T. Goals Made Simple.* Archangel Ink.

Dream, Goal(s), and Plan of Action

(Below are some example questions to help get you started. The following pages consist of a few worksheets, which you can use, as you wish.)

Dream:

- Why are you alive?

- How will you be remembered?

- What does the ultimate manifestation of your desired destiny look like to you?

Goal(s):

- What accomplishments would you like to achieve?

Plan of Action:

- What can you do right now to start moving in the direction of your dreams?

- What steps do you need to take to accomplish your goals?

- Do you need to develop any skills?

- Do you need to further your education?

Do what you can, with what you have, where you are.

-THEODORE ROOSEVELT

DREAM LIFE:

LIFE GOALS:

Short-term life goals:	*Long-term life goals:*
•	•
•	•
•	•
•	•
•	•
Plan of action:	*Plan of action:*
☐	☐
☐	☐
☐	☐
☐	☐
☐	☐
☐	☐
☐	☐

DREAM CAREER:

CAREER GOALS:

Short-term career goals:	*Long-term career goals:*
•	•
•	•
•	•
•	•
•	•
Plan of action:	*Plan of action:*
☐	☐
☐	☐
☐	☐
☐	☐
☐	☐
☐	☐
☐	☐

DREAM RELATIONSHIP(S):

RELATIONSHIP GOALS:

Short-term relationship goals:	*Long-term relationship goals:*
•	•
•	•
•	•
•	•
•	•
Plan of action:	*Plan of action:*
☐	☐
☐	☐
☐	☐
☐	☐
☐	☐
☐	☐
☐	☐

DREAM HEALTH:

HEALTH GOALS:

Short-term health goals:	*Long-term health goals:*
•	•
•	•
•	•
•	•
•	•
Plan of action:	*Plan of action:*
☐	☐
☐	☐
☐	☐
☐	☐
☐	☐
☐	☐
☐	☐

Take Action

Developing your dream(s), goal(s), and plan of action will depend on what you choose to do with your life. There will be certain skills or things you will need to do or learn in order to achieve your goals. Learning is a choice. No excuses. We can learn anything we want if we are willing to put in the effort and energy to do so.

Remember Natural Law 1: "Pure Potentiality"

"It's all a state of mind." Have you ever heard that before? It's true. So, make sure you have a positive state of mind and believe in learning and growth. It takes patience and practice. Be fearless. If you're a person that is trying to better yourself, you're on the right track.

Remember ...

- *Step 1*: Develop the Right Mindset

- *Step 2*: Learn Transcendental Meditation

- *Step 3*: Get a Vedic Astrology (Jyotish) reading and take a personality test

- *Step 4*: Decide what you want!

Sobriety brings clarity.

There is no need to worry about what others will think of you and your dreams. Remember they are "your" dreams and goals, not anyone else's. Others will have opinions, but remember in the end, it is you that will have to live with your Self. Focus on your Self and what you are doing, and you will be alright. So, if you have a dream, you have to find the courage to create it. It is all within you. You can do it!

You may not always be able to control what you think or feel, but you can learn to control how you act. Let others think what they will. That's not in your control. They will see for themselves. Besides, actions speak louder than words. So, once you decide what it is you want, take action. Take the steps you create for your Self in accomplishing your goals. Whether you need to learn or master a skill, give a speech, write a book, take a new job, get in shape, find something you love, learn to meditate, and so on. Have the courage to face your fears and just go with the flow of what feels right for you. It will all work out.

Procrastination is the killer of most dreams. Not failure.

Just Do It!

-NIKE

Be Practical

Being practical is difficult for dreamers who love to imagine things beyond this world. I know; I am one of those dreamers. However, you can be practical in accomplishing your dreams if you take the steps in front of you at each moment. That is all you can do anyway. Focus on what is here and now. Win the moment!

Imagine you're at the bottom of a staircase. How will you get to the top? The practical solution is to take, "One step at a time." This book is a combination of practicality and spirituality. I began my journey seeking to know God. I wanted to be a writer/rapper/actor, but sometimes dreaming of how that would come about was too difficult for me to see all at once.

So, I chose to develop my daily routine around the healthy habits I'd learned including meditation, eating a balanced organic vegetarian diet, exercising daily, writing and reading. Try to do what feels right for you.

If you find that you have a hard time keeping your feet on the ground (as I did) because your head is always spinning with thoughts and ideas, listen closely. There are certain things you can do to ground your dreams into physical reality; it just takes time. You can reap what you sow, but sometimes the real big dreams take a little longer.

For instance, if you plant two different seeds at the same time; let's say a lettuce seed and an apple seed. The lettuce seed will grow and provide a vegetable in two to three weeks. The apple seed, however, will take three to four years for a small tree to grow and up to eight years for a full-sized apple tree reaching twenty-feet tall.

Although some seeds or ideas can be planted at the same time, they don't all grow or blossom at the same rate. Some require more time, effort, and energy to generate more bountiful fruit. So, it is important to be patient and practical with your actions. The word practical stems from the Greek word *practice*. I also think it closely resonates with the word *tactical*. Therefore, I came up with the saying: "Being practical, is practicing tactical action."

It is also important to remember that if you build a castle in the clouds, you need to build a solid foundation and staircase from where you are to get there. Don't be afraid to dream big. What is it you can do today to grow closer to achieving your goals?

Finding Solutions

So, you found your dream. But there are other things preventing you from achieving them. What are those things? Are they physical blocks like a job, a certain amount of strength you wish to achieve, a physical skill you want to develop? Are they mental or emotional blocks like doubt or fear? Many times, these things are intertwined.

First, we need to identify the problem. If you want to publish a book you first need to finish writing the book. Then, find the money to publish and market it. You will probably need a certain amount of time to finish the book and a job to make money so when the book is finished you can publish it.

Many times, finding solutions is the easy part but following through is what people struggle with. Due to the ever-changing human emotions we experience, our perspective can change many times throughout the course of a day, a week, a month, a year, five years, ten years, a lifetime, and so on. Finding stability in some routine can help maintain structure in your life and help keep you on the "right track."

This is a solution in itself. Structure. Organize your mind. Prioritize your life.

This will help you see all other problems more logically and find solutions and plans of action to solve them effectively. This problem-solving ability develops naturally with more exposure and experience to situations in life or in meditation. You can start to see beyond obstacles whether those obstacles are abstract or concrete.

- Do you want to do music? Take music lessons. Listen to music. Practice music.

- Do you want to be an athlete? What sport? Start training. Eat healthy. Practice.

- Do you want to develop ideas into more practical theories? Take a class in philosophy. Read more books. Find a mentor. Go back to school.

- Do you want to be an astronaut? Learn what it takes to be an astronaut, and then do it.

You can do anything! Just decide and develop your plan of action.

And don't believe people who project their own doubts and fears onto you. Just because someone is older than you, doesn't mean they are more intelligent than you. It's wise to respect your elders but be careful not to let their opinions influence you negatively. This takes a good amount of discernment to understand the difference between someone else's projection and valuable advice.

Win the Moment!

Every moment is a gift.

When inspiration and opportunity strike, we need to be able to act on it.

Break it down. What can you do right now?

To climb a mountain, you first need to get off the couch.

Every book starts with a single word.

You don't have to write the whole book today; just start with one word, one sentence, one paragraph, one page.

You can watch as many inspirational videos as you want, but if you don't get up off the couch, it won't matter.

If you want to achieve your vision, then you need to act on the thoughts that inspire you. Now! It's like trying to start a fire. Once you get a spark that is burning a little bit you need to feed the fire in order for it to keep burning. So, if and when the spark of inspiration strikes, you need to act on it in order to fuel that inspirational fire. The more consistently you do this, the more effortless it becomes to understand and do repeatedly.

Real inspiration will spark something in you to take action. Now. Not later.

The moment you feel inspiration strike, you need to take immediate action. Follow the thoughts that inspire you. Trust yourself to take the steps to do what you're inspired to do. Trust the creative impulse.

For me, it comes down to self-talk. When I get a thought that inspires me, I trust and act on it. I usually say in my head, "Here we go!" And then, I surrender to the stream of consciousness that wants to come through me. I've gotten better at this because I practice it. You can too.

When you feel that spark—act on it. Then, surrender to the flow. Even if it's just writing or drawing something that you feel inspired to. If you're busy and can't follow the impulse right then, at least take a moment to stop and allow that seed of inspiration to be planted with a little tender love and care. Make a note of it. Take the action necessary to plant the seed so you can come back to it when you have more time to commit to it.

What can you do right now?

Doubt and Fear

Doubt: To be uncertain about; consider questionable or unlikely; hesitation to believe; to distrust.

Fear: A distressing emotion aroused by impending danger, evil, pain, and so on, whether the threat is real or imagined.

Overcoming your doubts and fears depends on what you doubt or fear—if you are doubting your Self or another person or God; if you fear a performance or judgment by your peers. Whatever you're doubting or fearing, there are things you can use to overcome those doubts and fears, which will help you to believe in your Self or others or God.

The answers depend on the questions. Learning to meditate can help become more inquisitive so you can learn to ask the right questions. Not just to get an answer, but to gain a better understanding.

Trust your preparation. If you're an athlete, trust your techniques and all the drills you've practiced preparing you for your game. If you're a rapper or singer, trust that you've recited your songs so many times that you know all of the words by heart. If it's a big test, trust that you've studied enough to pass with flying colors. But remember, you do have to actually practice. You have to put in the effort. You have to walk the walk.

If you doubt other people, communicate with them. State why you're uncertain or questioning them. This might clear up any confusion. If it's God you doubt, then communicate with Him or Her if that's who God is to you. Ask for clarity about whatever it is that's causing you to feel doubt or fear. Ask and then listen.

Pray to talk to God. Meditate to listen to God.

Named must your fear be before banish it you can.

-YODA

Fear is the path to the dark side. Fear leads to anger, anger leads to hate, hate leads to suffering.

-YODA

Train your Self to let go of everything you fear to lose.

-YODA

What are your Fears and Obstacles?

What are your fears and obstacles?	
Fears:	Obstacles:

How can you overcome them?

How can you overcome them?	
Fears:	Obstacles:

What Is, Not What If...

Choose to focus on what Is. Don't worry about what if...

"What If" is in your imagination. It is an illusion of one of an infinite number of possibilities.

Focus on what Is. And that will allow you to act more effectively right now.

In order to do so, you need to be free of memories from the past and fantasies of the future.

Focus on what Is ... right now.

Allow your Self to be right here. Right now. Surrender.

You are always being guided. Everything is guiding you to where you need to be, but this only becomes clear in the present moment. It becomes an experience that builds your faith and furthers your understanding of what the present moment Is.

We are here. We are now.

What is it that you need to learn?

Freedom from fear.

Acceptance. Letting go of control.

Allowing your Self to Be...

The present moment. Pure Consciousness. Absolute Being.

That Is It.

You. Are. That.

Tat tvam asi. (Thou art that)

Aham brahmasmi (I am totality)

Hallelujah, Amen.

Bliss consciousness.

Consistency and Commitment

Once you make your decision and write down your dream(s), goal(s), and plan of action, you must stay on course. "Practice tactical action." You must consistently work toward your goals and make a commitment to follow through. Discern where to invest your "effort and energy." Developing a scheduled routine is a good way to stay focused on your goals and eliminate distractions. If you have to work another job, attend school, take care of your family, or spend time doing other things that is alright, it is part of life. Using a time management sheet to help block off chunks of time to pursue your goals can help if you have a busy schedule.

Being able to commit to your goals and eliminate all distractions when you're attempting to pursue them is also important. If you're a writer and have a favorite spot to write, make time to go there. But if you find that you're easily distracted by certain things, like TV, video games, or people then you need to remove those distractions.

For me, it changes. At first, I used to write in the silence of my room, but then I got sucked into Netflix and lost a lot of time. For a while, I went to a local café to write. Now, I can write wherever I choose to be free of distraction. Some days, I prefer my office; some days, I prefer to be outside in the park. Even if you only have time to commit one hour a day right now, that is a start.

Rome was not built in one day.

-JOHN HEYWOOD

Desire is the key to motivation, but it's determination and commitment to an unrelenting pursuit of our goal—a commitment to excellence—that will enable us to attain the success we seek.

-MARIO ANDRETTI

STEP 5:
STAY COMMITTED!
KEEP GOING!

Sometimes, You Gotta Do What You Gotta Do!

After recording a rap album, I realized that some days I liked my music and other days I didn't. I realized my music was a way to express and process my emotions, but the feeling of emotions is fleeting. I wanted to write something from a higher perspective, not just from emotionalism because emotions are ever-changing. I'm grateful to have learned so much from writing songs; it was and still is one of the most therapeutic activities in my life.

A few years ago, I was broke and living at home with my parents and substitute teaching at my old high school, not my desired reality. My uncle Scotty ended up getting me a job as a construction superintendent, and after working almost sixty hours a week for about six months, I had enough money in my pocket and fire in my belly to say, enough is enough, and I stopped playing the victim in my life.

If I stayed in that position, I would've kept making money at the expense of my own happiness and dreams. If you're in a job that you don't love and it's miserable, I feel for you. If you want to find a job you love, it may take a tremendous amount of effort and energy to do so on your own. But remember, no one else will do it for you. You will need to take responsibility for your Self and have the courage to pursue your own dreams. You will have to decide how long you'll do what you don't love, before you say enough is enough.

This doesn't mean that you need to quit your job and completely devote your time to chasing your dreams. Sometimes, you've got to do what you've got to do, so you can do what you love to do. After six months of working as the construction superintendent, I made enough money to find a better job, and although it paid less, it was more aligned with my dreams and goals. I found a job as a professor, teaching a health-related fitness course and managing a recreation center. Now, I live in a beautiful apartment and have more free time to continue writing, making music, and pursuing acting more seriously, while still working at my job and meeting my basic human needs.

Much of what I teach is structured around the objective knowledge I've gained, but I also share my personal experiences and use my intuition to best help those I'm working with. My goal is to provide practical solutions that can be implemented to help others live happier, healthier, and more successful lives.

It's not "me." I'm not special. It's the organizing structure of intelligence that I surrender to daily, which works through "me." Truth, love, and knowledge. You want it? Learn to meditate. It will become clearer with time and practice.

Discernment

Discernment is how to decide through intuitive judgments where to invest your attention and energy. If you're doing something that is draining your energy and is not aligned with your goals, it's a sign that you should not be doing it. When you're doing something in alignment with your destiny, it should feel as if you are being guided and the energy just flows through you. There isn't much thought to it because it feels effortless and flows naturally.

It's like floating in a river with a strong current that carries you without having to swim. If you try to swim against the current of your own destiny, you will feel struggle and strain. If you surrender to the flow of the river or the Universe or God, you will be guided all the way.

This can come in many forms. For example, the distractions mentioned previously can prevent your flow of energy toward your destiny. I got into a conversation with someone who wanted to talk about something that I had no interest in, but he was very excited. I could feel my energy being sucked out and drained, so I politely disengaged from the conversation and returned to writing this section of the book.

Does everything happen for a reason? If I hadn't engaged in that conversation, would I have included this section of discernment into this writing? It was the actual experience that led me to a greater understanding. But I learned. What is it in your life that you're resisting? What is it you need to let go of?

Situations will arrive in life and you will have to discern or be aware of their influence on you. The greater your awareness, the easier it will be for you to discern what situations, people, experiences, foods, and habits are most beneficial for you and those that are not. Practice observational awareness.

Eventually, your perception will become so refined that you will be able to discern the potential for negativity and positivity in your very own thoughts. Your conscious awareness will guide you to better understand which thoughts are good for you and which ones are not. Eventually, you will be able to live from a state of "being" and recognize how thoughts and feelings are intertwined and how they come and go. You just observe and decide which ones to act on if you decide to act at all.

Have the courage to say yes, and the wisdom to say no.

-B. OAKMAN

STEP 6:
MAKE A SACRIFICE AND
STAY DISIPLINED!

Sacrifice and Discipline

Once you've made a commitment to your dream(s) and goal(s) and are following your plan of action, you may need to make certain sacrifices. This is not an easy thing to do. This is where discipline comes into play. Have the discipline to sacrifice some things to remain true to your dream(s)/goal(s). Try to understand the importance and the reason for your sacrifices.

I used and abused drugs and alcohol and suffered from depression and anger issues. If I never got sober and quit doing those things, you wouldn't be reading this book right now. I made the sacrifice and have maintained discipline in my practice of prioritizing sleep, meditation, sobriety, and writing.

In the space below this paragraph, write down the things you will sacrifice and the reason you need to sacrifice them. This may help you see the importance of the sacrifice. If it is your true dream(s) or goal(s) you're pursuing, you will understand the importance of making these sacrifices and have the discipline to stay on track. It's not always easy but it's a good way to remind yourself why you're making these sacrifices. If you get lost or fall off track that is alright, just get back up and get back on track. Learn and adapt.

Sacrifice:

Reason:

One day at a time.

-ALCOHOLICS ANONYMOUS

Time Management

Time Management							
Daily Schedule							
	Mon	Tue	Wed	Thu	Fri	Sat	Sun
5:00 AM							
6:00 AM							
7:00 AM							
8:00 AM							
9:00 AM							
10:00 AM							
11:00 AM							
12:00 PM							
1:00 PM							
2:00 PM							
3:00 PM							
4:00 PM							
5:00 PM							
6:00 PM							
7:00 PM							
8:00 PM							
9:00 PM							
10:00 PM							
11:00 PM							
12:00 AM							
1:00 AM							
2:00 AM							
3:00 AM							
4:00 AM							

PACE Your Self

Present—Being present in the moment allows the opportunity to accept what Is.

Acceptance—Accepting what Is allows you to see with more clarity.

Clarity—Seeing with more clarity allows you to evaluate with more precision.

Evaluation—Evaluating where you are, what you want, and why is a constant process to make the most informed decisions.

PACE yourself. One day at a time. One moment at a time.

Meditation. Contemplation. Observation. Reading. Writing.

Life itself is a process of knowledge and experience.

We all process our own experiences differently, but in general there are some keys to helping us unlock the infinite storehouse of knowledge within us.

All thoughts come from a source of infinite potential.

Contacting that source can be done in numerous ways, sometimes with effort and sometimes with ease, sometimes with intention, and sometimes spontaneously.

We all have the potential to access this world of wonder without drugs or years of meditation in the mountains of the Himalayas.

It's simple.

Sit and breathe. Meditate.

You will see in time.

Don't Forget Your DIAPER CAR

DIAPER CAR is an acronym for the keys to increasing motivation in pursuit of your goals.

- **D**irection—Goal/target/objective

Having a set goal/target/objective is the first and foremost important thing to increasing your motivation. What good is an archer without a target? Having a specific idea of what it is you want to achieve will allow you to find your direction.

- Intensity—Effort & energy/plan of action/skill development

  How quickly are you going to try and reach that target? How much effort and energy are you going to put into achieving that goal? If you need to learn a skill, how much time are you going to dedicate to learning that skill?

- Attitude—Mindset/learning/growth

  There is no failure. Just learning and growth. Keep learning. Keep growing. Keep going.

- Persistence—Patience/hard work/sacrifice/discipline

  How long are you willing to work toward your goal? When obstacles come and they will, what will you do? Give up? Or keep going? Learn to manage your time. Adapt to changes.

- Evaluate—Track your progress/strengths/weakness/adjust process.

  Evaluate your progress and your process. Find what works and build on it, find what doesn't work and change/eliminate it.

- Reflect—Reflect on what is now relevant to you. As you grow through life, your desires, ambitions, and priorities change. Reflect on what is important to you now.

- *Continue*—If your goal is still relevant to you and you want to continue, continue.

- Adjust—If your goal is still relevant but you're process needs adjusting or there is something else that needs to take priority right now, adjust.

- Redirect—If your goal is no longer relevant and you've identified a new goal that you wish to aim for, redirect.

You're the Only One with the Power to Change Your Self

We all have freewill and we will have to decide for ourselves when and if we want to change something about ourselves. I've spent a long time wanting and trying to change other people and things about the world in which I live. But I've accepted the fact that I can only change my Self, which will, in turn, influence others and the world.

At times, I find my Self wondering: Who am I to think that I know what is "right and good" for others? Then, I accept that I can only speak from my experience and what I have discovered that has helped me. I use the words "right and good," but they can also be substituted for life supporting, healthy, and beneficial.

So, how do I balance this desire to help others but not come off as preachy, self-righteous, arrogant, or overly critical? It's a process. I try to listen with compassion from a place of nonjudgment and unconditional love. If I offer advice, I try to use the word "could" instead of "should or would," implying more of an option for those I'm speaking with to choose for themselves. I try to share objective knowledge along with personal (subjective) experiences to help others see a different perspective that maybe they will relate to.

It takes a balance of objective knowledge and personal experience to convey a message that is holistic enough for individuals to really understand. I try to connect with people and share what I believe might be relevant. For me, it always comes back to loving and caring for people.

I try to ask the deeper questions that will help others make their own discoveries and then *listen*. Trying to get the messages of the mind and heart to coordinate and work together is ideal. More on listening later.

Self-Worth and Identity

This reflection of Self-Worth and Identity was inspired by my emotional response to a comment someone made to me. It triggered such deep reflection and psychological analyzation that I could no longer be around anyone and had to leave the situation immediately. Even after a car ride home and a twenty-minute meditation, I still had to reflect and write about this situation.

So, a group of three friends and I were sitting around playing a card game and listening to music, and I started imitating some mumble rapper that one of my friends liked. At this point in time, all these friends were aware that I'd been working on music since getting sober and had been recording raps for a few years, but I had gained no notable recognition from them. One of my friends asked, "Why are you making fun of him? Are you just jealous because he's famous and you're not?" Her comment immediately triggered something within me. Regardless of her intentions with that comment, it caused me to look at myself differently and eliminate being hurt again in the future by something like this. Not because I'd avoid people or control what other people said to me, but instead, I needed to identify and heal from the root cause of this issue.

The root cause was that I had placed my self-worth on the objective pursuit of becoming a famous rapper. I had attached my self-worth to a desired outcome. I had projected my self-worth onto an ideal identity. Once I was aware of this, I saw how silly it seemed. If my self-worth was based on anything other than my Self in the present, as I am, it created separation and apparent deficiency.

After I left that gathering and went home to reflect, I realized my self-worth should only be tied to my Self. No other measures are necessary. Self is being. Being is worthy. For example, you do not need to have, be, or do anything. Your existence is enough. There is nothing you need to do, be or achieve to be worthy. Your self-worth should be based solely upon your Self. Your Self is your soul. Your Self is your being. You are enough. You are worthy as you are. That is what I learned from this experience. And from that experience, I remembered how important self-talk is. Do we listen to and believe to be true what others think of us? Or do we trust our Self?

Self-Talk

Self-talk is what we say to ourselves in our own minds. It is important to eliminate negative self-talk. When negative thoughts enter your head, let them come and then let them go. And try not to entertain the negative thoughts. If the negative thoughts are overpowering then meditation, prayer, and positive self-talk can help.

But remember not to suppress your emotions. Allow yourself to feel your feelings but remember you don't have to attach to those feelings. Allow yourself to witness your thoughts come and go. They're just thoughts. Take a deep breathe. Return to your Self. Breathe.

It helps to have positive quotes and prayers handy as a reminder throughout the day. For example, my coffee mug has the *Serenity Prayer*, which reads:

God grant me the serenity to accept the things I cannot change

Courage to change the things I can

and the Wisdom to know the difference.

I use prayer as a way of consciously releasing the negative thoughts. Meditating does this more subtly over time with minimal effort. If you need to return to the section on prayers, go for it. Create your own if you want. Based on what you think you need help with. Try it out. See what works for you.

I am Healthy. I am Strong. I am Worthy. I am Willing. I am Ready. I am Able.

Other Examples of Positive Self-Talk and Positive Quotes

I Think I Can, I Think I Can, I Think I Can.

-THE LITTLE ENGINE THAT COULD

The height of our accomplishments is determined by the depth of our convictions.

-WILLIAM F. SCANAVINO

The greatness of a man is not in how much wealth he acquires but in his integrity and ability to affect those around him positively.

-BOB MARLEY

My Positive Self Talk:

We should combine these quotes. And see what happens.

We must learn to think positively and believe in ourselves. Only then will we be able to achieve our limitless potential and lead others on the same path to righteousness. Ha-ha ... Righteous Bro!

-DUSTIN MATTHEWS (TO BE DETERMINED)

Healing "Your" Inner Child

Talk to yourself. If you find you are in pain or suffering, try talking to yourself like you'd talk to a child you love and care about. You wouldn't be mean to that child, would you? You would have patience. You would have compassion. You would listen to them and help correct their perception.

Humans are like Russian Nesting Dolls with stored psychological trauma from past experiences. So even though I might be walking around in the strong, beautiful body of a 30-year-old Sigma Male, I have many layers.

I have a baby Dustin inside who wants nurturing all the time. He feels whiny and needy and just wants nurturing.

- Self-solution: *I need to nurture myself.*

- Self-talk example: *I love you, buddy. Shh. Shh. Shh. I love you, buddy.*

- Self-love example: *Hug myself. Hold myself.*

I have a little 3- to 7-year-old Dustin who wants attention all the time.

- Self-solution: *I need to validate and appreciate myself for the things I can do.*

Self-talk example: *You're doing a very good job, buddy. You're doing so well. You're very handsome and intelligent. You're very kind and compassionate. You're very talented and can achieve anything you set your mind to. I love you buddy. Keep working hard. But not too hard. You're enough no matter what you do or don't do. You're amazing, funny, kind, and loving. You're doing great, buddy!*

- Self-love example: *Make a list of all you've accomplished and overcome.*

  - You overcame alcohol and drug addiction.

  - You played and coached college football.

  - You have three degrees.

  - Listen to your music. Remember where you started. You're getting better.

  - You're writing a book.

I have a teenage boy inside of me between the ages of 13 to 17. This version of me is a virgin. He doesn't know much about sex except for the fact that it's all he thinks about other than sports. Sports and girls. Girls and sports. This *me* had his heart broken when his first real girlfriend who he idolized made out with three of his friends at a party. *Uh oh!* One of those friends was his "best friend." Now, this *teenage me* has trust issues; he doesn't think he deserves to be loved. Why would she cheat on him? He blames himself.

Now, he doesn't trust his friends. He doesn't trust anyone. The people he cared about most have hurt him the most.

- Self-solution: *This* me *needs to forgive and forget what happened in the past and learn to love himself. He needs to believe that he deserves to be treated better by his partners and friends and there is nothing wrong with him based on the actions of others.*

- Self-talk example: *My song. You deserve better.*

  This is the part of my inner child who I find needs the most counseling. He's old enough to start experiencing the real ups and downs in life and the pain that comes with growing up but has a limited understanding of what is really going on. He's trying to become a man, but his brain isn't fully developed yet. He'll need for you to be calm and patient but also disciplined and stable. He needs to talk about his feelings in order to understand them. This is how he'll develop emotional intelligence. (Girls are usually more emotionally intelligent because there isn't a social stigma about them talking about their feelings, but with boys/ men, it's portrayed in society as weakness.) But boys/men have feelings, too. And they need someone to talk to as well.

- Self-love example: *Find an outlet to express your feelings. Meditation. Therapy. Writing. Making music. Working out. Healthy Ego Development. Developing Skills. Accomplishing Goals. Anything that increases self-confidence and self-worth.*

The 19- to 23-year-old Dustin. Watch out, ladies. I'm not a virgin anymore. I'm playing college football and partying like a wild animal. Deep down, I'm in pain, but I'm building a strong wall around my heart because I've been hurt before emotionally and don't know how to deal with it, so I build my body to be strong, thinking that muscles will protect my feelings. I've been hurt by those I was closest to and numb myself to reliving those experiences in current relationships, but I'm not yet aware of that. I have a lot of random hookups but don't get involved in committed relationships because I still don't trust anyone. I'm the captain of the football team. I abuse drugs, alcohol, and sex. I had an affair with my professor, who was married with two kids. I'm obsessive and focus on gaining knowledge and doing well in school in an effort to end my suffering but feel an emptiness that nothing seems to fill. I almost overdosed. I met a girl whose name means, the "Light" and she became my inspiration to quit drinking, drugs, and abusing sex. She became my muse, but she lives in Spain, and we haven't seen each other since we first met when I was 23 years old—the year I started getting clean and sober.

- Self-solution: *Learn to heal your Self. Learn Transcendental Meditation.*

- Self-talk example: *It's time you learn to meditate. You need to learn to heal yourself. You have so much potential, but you need to heal yourself before you can share what you have to offer with others.*

- Self-love example: *At the age of 23, I quit drinking and doing drugs and started writing this book. At age 24, I learned the practice of Transcendental Meditation. Sleep, meditation, writing, working out, and eating healthy are my new habits, which allow me to love my self the way I need to be loved.*

The 23- to 29-year-old me. I'm done abusing drugs, alcohol and sex. I think I'm now ready to start looking for a long-term, committed relationship. I've been writing songs and books inspired by the muse in my life. I discovered a new muse that I could see a future with, but things didn't work out. Being in love with a woman who has a child and a ten-year relationship with her child's father brings new meaning to the term *quantum entanglement.* I continue to work on my career goals, but I feel like a mutually loving relationship will provide the deep love and connection I want in my life.

- Self-solution: *Prioritize and love your Self.*

- Self-talk example: *I trust the timing of God's plan and will be patient. I'm worthy of love, and when it's meant to be, it will be. I don't need to hold onto the women from my past because I trust if it is meant to be then it will be. I surrender to your will, God.*

- Self-love example: *Sleep, meditation, writing, working out, and eating healthy are my new habits, which allow me to love myself the way I need to be loved. Focus on the best version of yourself that you want to become for you. Not for anyone else.*

The 30-year-old present-day Dustin.

- Self-solution: *Surrender to the Will of the Divine. Trust your Intuition.*

- Self-talk example: *I want to be the best version of myself for everyone else. Okay, I surrender, God. I'm yours.*

- Self-love example: *Surrender to the Present.*

The future Dustin.

- Self-solution: *Be your authentic Self!*

- Self-talk example: *You're the man! You did it! Anything you wanted to do you've done! Look how much love and laughter you brought into this world.*

- Self-love example: *Be your authentic Self!*

Step 7: Keep Healing Yourself

Try this for yourself.

Get a piece of paper and write down the ages of your inner child that need healing. Talk to those versions of yourself by writing and using the Self-solution, Self-talk example, and Self-love bullets like above.

This can be as detailed as you need it to be. It is a good way to uncover those parts of your Self, which are still inside needing some attention and healing. It's pretty cool; once you heal these deeper parts of yourself, you will become happier and feel more whole and complete in your Self. Good luck!

Age of the inner child and trauma experienced:

Self-solution:

Self-talk example:

Self-love example:

Age of the inner child and trauma experienced:

Self-solution:

Self-talk example:

Self-love example:

Age of the inner child and trauma experienced:

Self-solution:

Self-talk example:

Self-love example:

Age of the inner child and trauma experienced:

Self-solution:

Self-talk example:

Self-love example:

Setting Boundaries

First and foremost: Find security in your Self.

When dealing with other people, there will be times when things are smooth and times when things can get turbulent.

Questions to consider when dealing with other people:

1. Is this person capable of seeing another point of view besides their own?

2. Is this person worth having hard, uncomfortable conversations with?

3. If you answered *yes* to both of these questions, reflect and set boundaries with clear examples of what acceptable and unacceptable behavior is if the relationship is to continue.

4. If no, goodbye. Sometimes, this approach can hurt people's feelings, so a little communication might be better than just "goodbye." But you get the point.

5. If you have to cut ties with someone, try to do it cordially to minimize damage to that person's feelings.

6. Once the boundaries are set, if they're broken again, repeat Steps 1 and 2.

7. If you have to repeat Steps 1 and 2 often, consider raising the bar about who you let into your life. Some people want to stay in hell. The comfort of their pain and suffering can be secure for them regardless of how it affects you.

8. It always comes back to … Find security and stability in your Self.

Stay in the Boat

In this world, imagine we're all floating around in the ocean. Some know how to swim. Others are drowning. There is a boat. That boat is knowledge.

Stay in the boat of knowledge.

But what if everyone I love is drowning around me? Shouldn't I jump in and save them?

Stay in the boat of knowledge.

If you jump in to save them, they will drag you down. Or others will see you saving them and try to be saved, too. Then, they will grab at you and drag you down.

Stay in the boat of knowledge.

Become a strong rower. Build ropes and flotation devices to throw out to them.

Stay in the boat of knowledge.

Throw out a float. Keep rowing. Eventually, if they smarten up, they'll swim over to the boat, get in, and help you row.

If you jump in, you'll drown with the rest of them.

Stay in the boat of knowledge.

What are floatation devices? Knowledge. Sobriety. Sleep. Meditation. Therapy. Exercise. Nutrition. You lead by example once you get your stuff together and by staying in the boat.

Health Is Wealth

It's important for us to take great care of our body, mind, and spirit because when we do, they will take great care of us. The three aspects of personal health we'll talk about now are: mental/emotional health, physical health, and spiritual health. If you want to become more successful, you will need to improve all three aspects of your personal health. Yes, it's that simple. The better you feel the more productive you will be. The calmer and more peaceful you are, the clearer you will be able to think, solve problems, and find the best solutions.

Learning about proper nutrition and exercise is essential. This means commitment and dedication will be necessary. It is a *lifestyle*.

- Ideally, you could try to get 7 to 9 hours of sleep each night.

- You could learn to breathe properly. In through the nose with your diaphragm or belly pushing out, and then out through the mouth while contracting the diaphragm or pulling the belly in.

- You could learn to hydrate properly. About 96 fl. Oz. water per day, ideally, no alcohol, and limit caffeine.

- You could learn to eat properly. Eat natural foods. Does is grow from the Earth?

- You could learn to exercise properly. Posture, yoga, cardio, and resistance training.

- You could practice Transcendental Meditation. This will benefit all areas of your life.

Our minds, bodies, and souls can withstand anything if we treat them properly. Ideally, you could prioritize your health and find what habits work best for you. It will take effort and experimentation. If you try these things in this book and practice them daily, over time, you will see positive change. But it is your life and your choice and responsibility. If you really want to, you can do it!

STEP 8:
PRIORITIZE SLEEP (IDEALLY 7 TO 9 HOURS A NIGHT)

Sleep

According to Matthew Walker, the author of *Why We Sleep*, sleep is a biological necessity for humans. I highly recommend reading his book or at least watching his Ted Talk titled: Sleep is Your Super Power.

So, what happens when we sleep?

Our bodies regenerate themselves during sleep. We are living organisms, made up of billions of living cells that are constantly living and dying. When we sleep, we allow our bodies to heal and repair itself. Have you ever seen someone who hasn't slept? They look like they're dying. That's because they haven't allowed their body to regenerate during sleep.

Our brains are like sponges. At night, when we sleep, our brain stores all the memories from that day and wrings out the water (knowledge/experience) in preparation for receiving more (knowledge/experience) the following day. Then, we wake up and go about our day soaking up more water (knowledge/experience). Not getting enough sleep at night can have a negative impact in many ways. We do not store as much of the water (knowledge/experience) from the previous day and will not be able to soak up as much water (knowledge/experience) the following day. There are many other negative side effects from a lack of sleep including, less testosterone, increased body fat, increased stress, a weakened immune system, and so on.

If this cycle continues, it has a snowball effect on our physiology and if we habitually do not get enough sleep, we are digging ourselves an early grave. Sleep should be the number one priority in all humans' lives every night. It is nature's best gift to the human race to heal ourselves. Utilize it (Walker, 2017).

Physical Exercise

Physical Exercise is one of the best ways to increase the natural production of dopamine in your brain. Dopamine is the brain chemical that makes humans feel "happy." Make sure you exercise daily. Balanced physical activity. Be careful not to overdo it.

After years of training as a college athlete and coaching college athletes, being a personal trainer and teaching health-related fitness at the university level, I have developed my own personal routine that works for me. This may not work for everybody due to a variety of factors including age and level of fitness, but the list below is a very general outline of the duration and type of exercise one should try to get each day.

At least 3 days per week:

- 20–30 minutes of cardiovascular exercise at your target heart rate. Your Target Heart Rate = 70% of your Max Heart Rate. Max HR is 220 – (Your Age). This type of activity includes walking, jogging, running, sprints, agility drills, jump rope, plyometrics, swimming, biking, rowing, hiking, etc.

- 20–30 minutes of resistance training. This means some type of muscular strength training. There are many exercises to choose from: deadlift, squat, power clean, hang clean, pull-ups, push-ups, burpees, ab work, curls, shrugs, lunges, etc.

- 2-3 Sets of 10-8-6 Reps of varying exercises from 50% max – 85% max. There is a more specific science to this but in general try to stick to these rules of thumb.

- 20–30 minutes of stretching. This includes yoga, dynamic stretching, static stretching, etc.

This is a general outline for the duration and types of exercise people should try to get. Feel free to do more if you want. I personally think it is best to do some sort of exercise every day rather than working out just two to three times a week, even if it is for a shorter duration and with less intensity. This will allow you to get into a consistent routine that your body will love. Do something active every day.

Weight Training 101

A Workout Sequence

- **1st: Warm-up:** A brisk walk or jog, jump rope, jumping jacks, abs, etc.

- **2nd: Dynamic stretch:** Walking lunges, power skips, high-knees, butt-kicks, shuffle, etc.

- **3rd: Explosive exercise:** Power cleans, hang cleans, plyometrics, agility drills, etc.

- **4th: Large muscle groups:** Squats, dead lifts, lunges, bench, rows, pull-ups, etc.

- **5th: Supplementary lifts:** Shoulder raise, bicep curl, triceps extension, shrugs, etc.

- **6th: Joint mobility/abs:** Shoulder pipe, hip mobility, wall ball stretch, abs, etc.

Terminology:

Rep: (Repetition) One complete motion of an exercise.

Set: A group of consecutive repetitions.

Weight: The unit of measurement used for how much of a load was moved.

Rest: The time in between sets to recover.

- Example: 3 sets of 10 squats with 135 lbs. and 30 seconds of rest in between each set.

Superset: Any group of two or more sets of different exercises done consecutively without rest in between.

- Example: 3 sets of 10 bench presses with 135 lbs. Superset with 3 sets of 10 pull-ups (body weight).

So, you would do your first set of bench presses and then immediately do 10 pull-ups. Then, rest.

Supersets are a great way to increase the intensity of your workout. There are also studies that suggest supersets are a great way to increase testosterone and growth hormone levels resulting in greater muscular endurance and strength.

Other Things to Remember

- **3-set rule:** Generally, doing 3 sets of an exercise will lead to "enough" work to make gains in muscular strength and endurance.

- **High reps vs. low reps:** Higher reps with lighter weight are generally for toning/endurance. Lower reps with heavier weight are generally for bulking/strength.

- **Volume:** Volume is a combination of how many muscles are worked, exercises done, sets, reps, and weight. Ideally, I try to do at least three full-body workouts per week.

- **Intensity:** The amount of work required for an activity. Often relates to the amount of weight being moved. I try to stay within 50–85% of my 100% max strength.

- **Frequency:** How many days per week or times per day you do these exercises? Finding a balanced routine is ideal.

- **Cross-training:** Trying different activities and engaging the muscles in different ways is a good way to engage the mind and body and keeps you from becoming bored.

- **Experience:** Start simple. Form first. If you're a beginner, start with light weights and learn proper technique. Best to do only body weight while young and developing. Weight training is safer to begin post-puberty. 12-13 years of age. Until then. Just body weight.

Healthy Eating

There are a lot of different diets out there. It is my belief that the most holistic and healthy diet comes from organically grown plant-based foods. If it doesn't grow from the earth, it is not natural and is therefore considered a processed food.

I recommend eating more leafy greens, legumes (beans), other fruits and vegetables as well as more nuts and seeds. The question I receive most often here is about protein. There is enough protein in legumes (beans) and nuts and seeds to meet the high protein needs of world-class athletes and bodybuilders along with the everyday person.

I also recommend looking into examples of superfoods such as avocados, blueberries, chia seeds, and so on. There is a wide variety of foods we could be consuming that are better for us, but these foods are not as commercialized as fast food or junk food. Here's a list of some healthy foods.

Leafy greens	Legumes/grains	Other veggies	Fruits	Nuts/seeds
Spinach	Green beans	Avocados	Apples	Almonds
Kale	Black beans	Cucumbers	Bananas	Cashews
Lettuce	Garbanzo beans	Celery	Oranges	Peanuts
Broccoli	Lentils	Beets	Tomatoes	Walnuts
Brussels sprouts	Kidney beans	Carrots	Grapes	Pine nuts
Cabbage	Quinoa	Sweet potatoes	Blueberries	Pumpkin seeds
Chard	Couscous	Squash	Strawberries	Sunflower seeds
	Brown rice	Zucchini	Watermelon	Flax seeds
	Oats	Cauliflower		Chia seeds
		Peas		

When it comes to nutrition for the human body; the analogy for fueling a gas-powered vehicle or machine works well. The three macronutrients or main nutrients that the human body needs are carbohydrates, proteins, and fats. The three key components that keep a vehicle or machine running are fuel (gasoline), oil, and the parts of the vehicle itself.

In this comparison, carbohydrates represent the fuel (gasoline) the vehicle uses. This is the primary source of our energy. Fats represent the oil that lubricates the parts of the machine and keep it running smoothly. Proteins maintain the parts of the vehicle itself, the frame or body of the vehicle.

Nutrition Advice to Those Who Are Interested

Simply put, we need to have a balanced intake of these three macronutrients to keep our vehicle (body) functioning properly. Depending on different body types and individual goals the ratios in which these nutrients should be consumed fluctuates.

- **Overall:** Eat more vegetables. Vegetarian complete protein sources: veggies/whole grains in combination with beans/

legumes/nuts/seeds. Healthy fat sources: avocado, nuts/seeds, beans/legumes, olive oil. Drink more water: 8–12 oz. glasses a day.

- **Eliminate:** Refined carbohydrates (bread, pasta, cake, cookies, pizza), trans-fats (deep-fried foods), processed foods, sugar, meat, and drugs/alcohol.

Goal-dependent advice: In combination with the above advice, the following are some more specific strategies that can help you reach your goals.

- *Muscle gain:* Along with a regular physical activity routine that includes at least three days a week of resistance training, an increase in total caloric intake is necessary to maintain and build muscle mass. Eating more meals throughout the day is the best way to keep your muscles fed and in an anabolic state. Eating something small every 2–3 hours that consists of at least 20 grams of protein and some carbs and fats is ideal. This is dependent on goals and the extent of your exercise routine. The best way to chart this is with a nutrition journal. Keep track of what you're eating and when you're eating it along with your exercise routine and evaluate and adapt as you go. In general, you should try to eat 1 gram of protein for every pound of your body weight. (Ex. A 200 pound man should consume 200 grams of protein a day to optimize muscle growth)

- *Fat loss:* Along with a regular physical activity routine that includes at least three days a week of cardiovascular endurance exercise, a decrease in total caloric intake will be necessary to start dropping some weight. You don't want to eliminate all of your calories at once. Take inventory of what you're consuming in a nutrition journal and start implementing small changes. Eliminating refined carbs such as bread and pasta can be a big change to your system and so you will need to consume more vegetables/legumes to compete with the amount of total calories your body was used to getting from refined carbs. Increasing your intake of proteins and fats can help you feel fuller longer, which then helps reduce cravings for carbs. If you feel fatigued, tired, and depressed try eating some fruit. Fruit has natural sugars, which can act in a way that increases blood sugar levels when feeling fatigued. Adding some peanut butter or something with higher protein/fat content with a piece of fruit can help balance out the blood sugar. Too much fruit, however, will just turn to fat, so be aware (Keane, 2017).

Conscious Eating

It's important to mention that the consumption of nutrients and knowing the breakdown of macronutrients you should be consuming is the grossest level of understanding. It's also important to understand which foods consist of carbohydrates, proteins, and fats, and balance your consumption based on your individual physiology and specific goals. For, the best results track your consumption and make the desired changes.

On a deeper level, it is important to be conscious of what you're consuming while you're consuming it. One of the main causes of the most prevalent health issues today, such as heart diseases, obesity, and diabetes, is the overconsumption of sugar, refined carbohydrates, meat, and processed foods. To protect yourself from these diseases, it's best to take preventative measures before it's too late. You can do this by expanding your knowledge of what you consume, what is actually in what you consume, and what state you are in when consuming it.

Have you ever heard of emotional eating? How about comfort food? As humans, we have a sensitive emotional body that can lead us to have lingering feelings (feelings that persist even after we think we have dealt with them) or feelings that we are not always conscious of if not managed properly. Holding onto the stresses of life, whether it is a conscious behavior or unconscious behavior, can lead to things like emotional eating and overconsumption in an attempt to heal emotional pain that we are avoiding or don't even know exists.

This is where conscious eating comes in. I've been experimenting with conscious eating for about five years now. Before consuming food, I take about thirty seconds or a minute to close my eyes and breathe and internally express my gratitude for the food. This helps to settle my emotions, so that I don't get into the habit of trying to sooth my emotions with food. If I am feeling emotions, I try to meditate for a few minutes before eating to avoid getting into the habit of using eating as a coping mechanism.

I also try to eat without doing anything else. I try to avoid eating while watching TV as this creates a separation in my conscious mind, and then I have a tendency to overeat. I realize this takes discipline but depending on your goals and if you really want to make a change, you have to take responsibility for your actions.

I know you can do it because I've done it. And if I can do it, anyone can. About three months after I quit drinking and doing cocaine, I had an internship at the University of Maine in Orono with their strength and conditioning coach, to help train their football players over the summer. Workouts started at 6 a.m. and went to about 8 a.m., and then I'd have the rest of the day off.

At the time, I was living at my parents' lake house, which was about thirty minutes from Bangor, which had a casino. I started going there every day after the morning training to play blackjack. I started the summer with $500 and then learned how to count cards. It's actually easier than you might think. But I don't recommend gambling.

After about two weeks of counting cards playing blackjack, I was up to about $5,000 and really excited that I was doing so well. I'd sit and play blackjack for hours and when the count was in my favor, I bet big and sometimes got lucky. But for three days in a row, I was very unlucky and lost everything. I lost $5,000 in three days and felt the addict in me come alive again. I had just switched my addiction, from alcohol and cocaine to gambling.

That night, I drove back to my parents' lake house crying and before I got there I stopped and bought two pizzas and two pints of Ben & Jerry's ice cream. I lay on the couch watching a movie, eating pizza and ice cream before crying at how hopeless I thought I had become. But I made it out of that, and if you're there so can you.

I realized that I have an addictive personality and it doesn't matter what it is; I can become addicted to anything—alcohol, drugs, gambling, food. I also realized that addiction was just my best way at dealing with deeper issues like depression, anxiety, and repressed trauma that I wasn't even consciously aware of at the time. This realization was a lot to handle but over time, I quit gambling and overeating.

So, try conscious eating. Try conscious living. Take care of your emotions. Take responsibility for yourself and your life. It can be hard at first, but it will lead you to feeling healthier and happier. Health and happiness go hand-in-hand.

Increase Your Resilience

The mind is a great tool. We need to learn how to use it effectively and efficiently. Being able to control your mind so it doesn't control you is essential. It takes practice, patience, and discipline. Transcendental Meditation. Did you learn it yet? It's probably the most beneficial tool to have in your tool belt for bettering your Self.

The body is a great vehicle and tool to use for numerous things as well. It is a vehicle that we temporarily inhabit to grow and reach higher states of consciousness. We are all here to evolve. It is important to keep our minds, body, and spirit healthy, rested, and active.

To increase and raise our physical, mental, social, and emotional resilience, there are a few things you can do. There is a Ted Talks video on YouTube by Amy Cuddy called *Our Body Language Shapes Who We Are*. This video speculates on the importance of body language. There is another Ted Talks video on YouTube by Jane McGonigal called *The Game That Can Give You 10 Extra Years of Life*.

On a daily basis, I raise my hands high over my head because this boosts physical resilience by increasing testosterone levels and snap my fingers exactly fifty times to boost mental resilience and willpower. To boost emotional resilience, look out a window or at an image of a baby or baby animal. To boost social resilience, shake someone else's hand or hug them for six seconds or send someone a quick thank you. This has been proven by research but for more specifics, visit: The Game That Can Give You 10 Extra Years of Life.

As you are aware, I also practice Transcendental Meditation regularly to benefit my spirit, which I believe feeds into all the rest. Consciousness is primary. Spirit first. They're one and the same.

Mental Attributes

- **Mental toughness**—Ensure that you stay mentally strong, live in the present moment, and embrace whatever it may bring. Whether it is pain or pleasure, victory or defeat. Choose to live in the present moment with an open heart and mind. Try not to let the negativity of others affect you. Control what you can control and let go of what you can't.

- **Knowledge**—Active listening. Engage. It is important to ask questions. Not just to get an answer, but to gain a better understanding. To gain a better understanding about something, you must choose the right questions to ask. Why? How? What? An open mind can receive Knowledge. Open your mind. Become receptive to knowledge, like a sponge.

- **Memory**—In the traditional western educational system, there are a lot of things to remember. This is called objective knowledge. Studying is a way to help you remember, know, and understand. A simple technique for memorizing is the use of flash cards. They can be used for anything: math, history, English, health, sports, etc. Write it. Read it. Repeat it.

  - *Math*—On one side, write the problem: 4+4. On the back, the solution: 8.

  - *History*—On one side, write the State: Maine. On the back, the Capital: Augusta.

- *English*—On one side, write a word: Dustin Matthews. On the back, the definition: The most intelligent, handsome, loving man alive.

- *Health*—On one side, place an image of a food item: (picture of banana). On the back, its name: Banana.

- *Sports*—On one side, write a Play: 36. On the back, your job. FB: OZ Right, Aim for Ass of EMOL, Block first unblocked thing.

- **Attention to Detail**—There is a reason for everything you do. If you want to be great, you need to put your attention into the details. They will build upon each other. It is a constant battle, but you need to pay attention to the details. Greatness is the product of numerous small successes.

  What adds up to be more, 2×100, or, 2×2, 10 times?

  $2 \times 100 = 200$

  $2 \times 2 \times 2 \times 2 \times 2 \times 2 \times 2 \times 2 \times 2 \times 2 \times 2 = 2,048$

  Small successes add up. Keep plugging away. Each day is an opportunity.

Learning Styles

A learning style is like a medium between knowledge and understanding. For some, one style may work wonderfully and for others it may not work well at all. It is different for everyone, but everyone has the ability to learn.

- **Aural**—The auditory or musical style prefers to use sound and music or listening to lectures and audiobooks.

- **Logical**—The mathematical style prefers to use logic, math, equations, reasoning, and systems.

- **Physical**—The kinesthetic style prefers to use the body and be hands on.

- **Social**—The interpersonal style prefers to learn in a group setting with others where they can talk about what they're learning.

- **Solitary**—The intrapersonal style prefers to work alone and study alone.

- **Verbal**—The linguistic style prefers to use words in speech or writing.

- **Visual**—The spatial style prefers to use pictures, videos, and space.

- **Transcendental Meditation**—Self-reflection, self-knowledge, subjective knowledge, super learning.

If you want to learn a complex skill, you must first make a commitment of at least twenty hours of practice. That is the amount of time that it takes to get "good enough" at something. To "master" a skill requires 10,000 hours of practice. But it is possible with practice, patience, and commitment to master a skill and doesn't take as long as you might think to become competent at performing that skill. Commit to twenty hours. You will surprise yourself.

Every individual has a different learning style. Some people are able to tap into all of the different learning styles. It is best to blend learning styles together to become more of a dynamic well-educated society. So, for students trying to learn, keep learning, keep trying. For teachers trying to teach, keep learning, keep trying, keep teaching.

We May Not Know the Ripples of Our Destiny

I'd like to share a story. I've spent a long time trying to get a glimpse of what the future holds for me. I pray to God to show me what my purpose is. Why am I alive? But from what I've experienced, we are guided to the things we need when we need them and it's not always what we might think.

I tend to have an overactive imagination, which is why I have learned to channel my energy into writing. But one day like any other, I was questioning my destiny. I was driving to the lake with my friend, telling her about how I was trying to find purpose in my life, when we passed the parking lot at the lake. There was a parked van, and a woman was standing outside it. I could see into the front seat and it looked like there was a fire in the center console.

I pulled in and parked, and by this time the flames were pouring out the driver's side window and the woman was about ten feet away kneeling down playing in a puddle. My friend and I were in shock that she was so oblivious. I jumped out of my car and yelled to her, "Hey, you know your car's on fire?"

She jumped up, ran to the van, opened the side sliding door, reached in and pulled out a child that had apparently been in the backseat the whole time. It was a little girl who was about two or three, and luckily the mother got her out in time, and she hadn't been burned or anything. The little girl was crying and looked terrified. Then out of nowhere, the father ran over screaming, "My daughter's in there." After their family reunited, they all started running away down the trail. This was the weirdest part. There was no exchange between them and us and they just fled the scene.

My friend and I called the fire department; we couldn't believe what we'd just witnessed. We wondered if the van was stolen or if they were on drugs or something, but we also wondered what would have happened if we hadn't pulled in at that exact time. Would the little girl have died in the fire? The point of the story is this: We may not know our destiny or the ripples our actions will have on the lives of others. What if that little girl goes on to become the president of the United States?

So, no matter where you are or what you are doing, have faith. You are important. You play a role in this universal adventure. You have and will continue to make an impact on the people and environment around you. It's important to reflect and decide what you want that impact to be. Choose carefully. Choose with care. Choose with love.

STEP 9:
FIND A CREATIVE OUTLET!

Creativity

Creativity is where intelligence and imagination meet. Practice it. Find creative solutions for problems. Or just use your creativity in whatever way you please, whether it is drawing, painting, playing an instrument, dancing, rapping, writing, singing, business or technological innovation, or just being yourself.

Finding an outlet for creative expression can be one of the most beneficial ways for individuals to learn and grow. Creative outlets can provide an opportunity to express yourself and gain a better understanding of the objective knowledge you are studying as well as the subjective knowledge of being actively engaged and aware of your own creative process. It can add purpose and meaning to your life.

For me, it was creativity and the pursuit of my creative hobbies that gave me a reason to live in times of darkness. There was a time when emotion and confusion ruled my mind and finding a creative outlet for that emotion allowed me to express it in a healthy way. It helped me work through my emotions rather than denying myself the permission to have feelings and expressing them.

The suppression of my emotions was one of the main causes of my depression, drug and alcohol abuse, and "bad" decisions in life. Emotional intelligence can be learned in many ways, meditating and allowing yourself to feel your feelings and having a creative outlet is essential.

I now realize how important it was for me to get those emotions out. Creative outlets allow you to release energy, negative energy needs to be released or transmuted. If you don't release the negativity and express it in some way, it stays within you, which just causes more pain and suffering.

This doesn't mean you have to record a rap album. There are many creative outlets for people to choose. Writing, singing, music, dance, acting, woodworking, car fabrication, tattoo artists, painting, business ideas, technology, and so on. But having an outlet for your emotions is critical.

If you want to check out my webpage where I share more of the creative content I'm developing go to: www.dustinmatthewsmedia.com

Below are some of my Album Covers.

What's in My Head? What's in My Heart?

What's in my head this morning? What's in my heart this morning? Do I stay in my head to avoid what's in my heart? She's gone. I don't want to feel about her anymore, so I obsess over a different creative project—finishing my book. It requires me to think about something other than her. Is that avoidance or is it healthy? Who decides? Me? You? A therapist?

I guess it is what it is. I'm not avoiding my feelings. I accept them as they come, but I'm done attaching myself to them and drowning in them. It's a fine line. I could return to the memories and replay them, stirring up some emotional hell and write another sad song about my longing for her. But I'm trying to change my story. I'm trying to change my beliefs. It's simple to think about beliefs on the surface. I believe this. I don't believe this.

But feeling and beliefs can sometimes be so deeply rooted and hard to let go of or even recognize that you're holding onto them in the first place. Sometimes, our beliefs are habitual, and breaking a belief is like uncovering a psychological trauma, which you now realize left a deep impression and caused you to believe something about yourself that is not necessarily true.

This can be called a self-discovery, or a revelation.

How does it happen? Self-awareness. Self-reflection. Self-acceptance. Self-inquiry. Meditation. Contemplation. Writing. Reading. Integrating knowledge and experience.

What do I believe about myself?

I'm self-aware. I'm self-reflective. Meditation, contemplation, reading, and writing help me learn. I'm intelligent. I'm compassionate. I'm healthy. I'm handsome. I'm sexy. I'm attractive. I'm caring. I'm creative. I'm funny. I've got three degrees. I played and coached college football to the best of my ability. I care. I try. I love deeply. I can write songs that move me and help me heal from my experiences. I want to help people.

- Try this for your Self. What do you believe about your Self?

- Allow your Self to speak/write from your heart. You may feel the shift as you think in your head. What's in my head? What's in my heart? Allow the two to coexist together.

What do you believe about your Self?

Quotes on Learning/Knowledge

The true sign of intelligence is not knowledge but imagination.

-ALBERT EINSTEIN

Conceive it! Believe it! Achieve it!

-NAPOLEON HILL

All our knowledge begins with the senses, proceeds then to the understanding, and ends with reason. There is nothing higher than reason.

-IMMANUEL KANT

Real knowledge is to know the extent of one's ignorance.

-CONFUCIUS

To know is to know that we know nothing. That is the meaning of true knowledge.

-SOCRATES

Opinion is the medium between knowledge and ignorance.

-PLATO

Live as if we were to die tomorrow. Learn as if we were to live forever.

-MAHATMA GANDHI

I've learned that people will forget what we said, people will forget what we did, but people will never forget how we made them feel.

-MAYA ANGELOU

Tell me and I forget. Teach me and I remember. Involve me and I learn.

-BENJAMIN FRANKLIN

There is no end to education. It is not that we read a book, pass an examination, and finish with education. The whole of life, from the moment we are born to the moment we die, is a process of learning.

-JIDDU KRISHNAMURTI

Human behavior flows from three main sources: desire, emotion, and knowledge.

-PLATO

I like to listen. I have learned a great deal from listening carefully. Most people never listen.

-ERNEST HEMINGWAY

Education is what remains after one has forgotten what one has learned in school.

-ALBERT EINSTEIN

Life's a dance we learn as we go. Sometimes, we lead and sometimes we follow.

-JOHN MICHAEL MONTGOMERY

All our knowledge has its origins in our perceptions.

-LEONARDO DA VINCI

He who seeks contentment never finds it. He who Is, does.

-DUSTIN MATTHEWS (TO BE DETERMINED)

Knowing what, brings us knowledge. Knowing how, brings us understanding. Knowing why, brings us peace.

-DUSTIN MATTHEWS (TO BE DETERMINED)

STEP 10:
KEEP LEARNING!

The Intangibles

- **Courage**—We must be full of courage. Remember the connection between courage and faith.

> *Men don't follow titles; they follow courage.*
>
> -WILLIAM WALLACE (BRAVEHEART, MEL GIBSON)

- **Determination**—Never give up. Surrendering is not the same as giving up.

> *Quitting when you have failed is failure. The only way to succeed is to keep trying.*
>
> -DUSTIN MATTHEWS (TO BE DETERMINED)

- **Pride/honor**—We represent ourselves, our families, and all of humanity. How do we want to be remembered?

> *How we do anything, is how we do everything.*
>
> -T. HARV EKER

- **Heart**—It's beating in your chest, pumping blood through your whole body. It's the reason you're alive. What are you going to do with the life it has given you?

Nothing is impossible to a willing heart.

-JOHN HEYWOOD

- **Love**—It is the most powerful emotion inside of you and in the Universe.

Love without a limit.

-DUSTIN MATTHEWS (TO BE DETERMINED)

Vision

The power of visualization is amazing and beautiful if you can learn to use it properly. Practice visualizing things you desire, things you want to happen, and the person you want to be. Visualize the big picture of what you really want and feel as if you've already accomplished it and hold that feeling in your heart. You can practice visualizing things that you want to happen any time. If you are in school or at work, try to focus on your studies or work. If you can't control this, it is called "daydreaming" and can negatively affect your studies or work life.

Once you have better control of your mind, you can visualize things you want to happen. You will be able to visualize the outcome of certain situations. Run through the situation in your mind and visualize the performance and results you desire. Try to *feel* the feelings you want to feel when these things happen. Make sure to use the power of your visualization for good and be careful what you wish for.

I used to use visualization for sports. I'd run through plays in my head for hours before falling asleep. Learn how to shut it off though, sleep is vitally important. Therefore, I suggest deciding upon a certain area or time of day to do this. I used to do it all the time, but it often prevented me from sleeping, so practice carefully.

It is easy to hate and it is difficult to love. This is how the whole scheme of things works. All good things are difficult to achieve, and bad things are very easy to get.

-CONFUCIUS

Practice does not make perfect. Only perfect practice makes perfect.

-VINCE LOMBARDI

Do Right.

-PAUL CASTONIA

Turn Your Desires Toward Your Own Heart

Keep your desire turning back within and be patient.

Allow the fulfillment to come to you.

Gently resist the temptation to chase your dreams into the world;

pursue them in your heart until they disappear into the Self, and leave them there.

It may take a little self-discipline, be simple, be kind, stay rested.

Attend to your own inner-health and happiness.

Happiness radiates like the fragrance from a flower and draws all good things towards you.

Allow your love to nourish yourself as well as others.

Do not strain after your needs of life—it is sufficient to be quietly alert and aware of them.

In this way, life proceeds more naturally, effortlessly.

Life is here to enjoy.

-MAHARISHI MAHESH YOGI

This takes a little practice and time to understand and apply. What helped me to better understand it was to imagine an invisible energy (my thoughts/ desires) that I was sending out into the world in an attempt to manifest my desire. I started redirecting that invisible energy inward toward my own heart. Every time I felt like my desires were pulling me out of my Self, I pulled that energy back into my heart. By doing this, I removed the separation between my desires and my experience.

Previously, I'd send my desires outward or project them and they continued to go outside of my Self, which left me feeling unfulfilled when they didn't come to fruition. So, I'd put more effort into thinking and trying harder and projecting harder. Thinking I needed to work harder, I needed to be successful. Push, push, push. Go, go, go. But that only caused me pain and suffering. By keeping my desires turning back into my own heart, they manifest in a way that is more natural and with minimal effort. By doing this, you bring your desires to you. You don't have to project them and make them manifest. You keep them close to your heart and they will manifest on their own.

I've been doing this recently, and the time between having a strong desire and pulling it back into my heart, to when it comes to fruition is almost seamless. There might be a few hours, a day or two but when Nature supports. *It* happens. Support of Nature is basically the Universe or God or The Cosmic Intelligence that underlies and supersedes all things. What I've discovered is surrendering to the expectation of *It* happening. It is not an intellectual understanding that makes *It* happen but a natural experiential feeling that may not be of conscious choice. It happens, when *It* happens. Keep your desires turning back within and be patient.

Reflect on your own experiences. Think of some of the best things in your life. Did you make it happen, or did it just seem to happen for you, and you were grateful that it did? You may have had the intention, but it's not always us who makes things happen. It's important to remember the process of preparation and putting in the work that we discussed earlier. Plant the seeds and nurture them. They will grow in their own time.

All things in life stem from Nature or God or the unseen realms. Trust in the unknown and have faith. If you feel as though you need to be in control of everything ask yourself "why?" Were you raised to believe that you had to try and control things to limit your suffering? Does being in control make you feel safer or more secure? Why? Ask yourself these questions. Take some time to consider your beliefs around control. How were you taught?

When we try to control what we cannot, we suffer or feel depressed and anxious. When we focus on the things we can control, we feel empowered. Consider these questions. What things can I control? What things do I need to surrender control of? How can I best act to manage the things that are within my realm of control?

- Can I control other people's feelings and behavior? *No.*

- Can I control my response to other people's feelings and behavior? *Yes.*

- Can I control how others perceive my actions? N*o.*

- Can I control my actions? *Yes.*

Place your focus on the things that you can control, and let God take care of the rest.

Self-Motivation

You need to be able to motivate yourself. You can't always rely on others to motivate you. You can find motivation in a lot of different ways from a lot of different things. Imagining the possibilities for the best person you can be in the future is a powerful and positive way to motivate yourself.

The future isn't here, the past ain't coming back. Take a look around man this is where we're at.

-DUSTIN MATTHEWS (TO BE DETERMINED)

Learn from the past and the mistakes you've made, but remember the past is in the past. Positive energy in your thoughts for the future is much more beneficial than letting the past eat you up inside and haunt you.

Finding certain images, quotes, or songs can boost your spirit and motivate you in a positive way. But remember that the positive energy is more beneficial than negative energy; in other words, choose love over hate and good over evil.

What is your deepest desire? Let that be your motivation.

Reflect On Your Own Intrinsic Motivation

Intrinsic motivation is motivation from within your own Self. Below is the key to increasing intrinsic motivation.

Need to feel: Autonomy, competency, and relatedness.

- **Autonomy**—The feeling of freewill. Like you have made the choice willingly.

- **Competency**—Having a required level or capacity of a knowledge/skill. Feeling like you're good enough or capable of doing what you desire to do.

- **Relatedness**—Feeling a connection, a reason. Feeling like your desire to do something will benefit others as well as yourself.

- In simpler terms, you must feel like you are choosing to do what you want, you are capable of doing it to the required level to be successful, and you do what you want for the benefit it will have on yourself and on others.

We all have something we were made to do. We just have to find what it is. And share it with the world.

-DUSTIN MATTHEWS (TO BE DETERMINED)

Leadership

Leaders aren't born; they are made. And they are made just like anything else, through hard work. And that's the price we'll have to pay to achieve that goal, or any goal.

-VINCE LOMBARDI

Whether we are talking about a family, a team, a school, a community, a state, a nation, or all of humanity, being a leader is a choice. It takes courage. It's not easy. It's hard. Not everyone wants to be a leader. But if you do want to be a leader, you need to lead by example. Some people choose to take the position of leadership; others are thrown into it. Either way, you must find the courage to lead.

There are two things to consider when talking about leadership. The first are leadership roles and the second are leadership qualities. But even if you are not in the position of a defined leadership role you still have the potential and ability to be a leader. There are all types of people that can provide leadership: parents, grandparents, aunts, uncles, siblings, cousins, friends, teachers, coaches, classmates, teammates, coworkers, neighbors, bosses, politicians, law enforcement officers, and people like you and me. You never know when you might be in a position to provide leadership or guidance.

If you are in a leadership position and you want people to trust your leadership, it's important to practice what you preach. It's hard to trust a hypocrite. It's also important to remember the first rule about intrinsic motivation. Whoever you are trying to lead has their own free will. They have to choose to follow you. You can lead a horse to water, but you can't make it drink. The horse will do so on their own if you have led it with a heart full of compassion, truth, and love.

Sometimes, it takes just as much courage to follow as it does to lead. There are times in life when you will need to find the courage to lead. There will also be times in life when you will need to find the courage to follow. I believe courage and faith are closely linked.

Leaders, we must have faith in our followers. Followers, we must have faith in our leaders. Leaders, we must provide our followers with hope. Followers, we must provide our leaders with hope. Leaders, we must have love for our followers. Followers, we must have love for our leaders. We're all in this together.

Honesty

- Stay true to your Self.

- Take responsibility.

- Speak the truth with compassion.

The truth will set you free.

-JESUS

Trust and love are essential within any relationship, family, team, community, state, nation, and all of humanity.

-DUSTIN MATTHEWS (TO BE DETERMINED)

Continue to Listen

Silence is the source. Silence is thy Self.

Tune into silence. This will cultivate receptivity and allow for a deeper understanding of your Self. With a deeper understanding of your Self, you can listen to others and interpret what is really going on with them. People can say a lot of things and use a lot of words but understanding what is under the surface requires you to listen.

- It's not always about what's being said.

- What's underneath what is being said?

- What's being felt? Use compassion and empathy to get a deeper understanding. Put yourself in their shoes with their beliefs to really gain an understanding of their perspective.

If you are in tune with silence, with truth, you can become a guide in the exploration of another's experience of Self. They will still have to make the choice. They need to be willing to explore and tune into their own silence, their own truth.

Silence is the great unknown of all that ever was, is, or will be. Some people fear the unknown and cling to what they think they know even if that is pain and suffering. They need to be willing to change. Listening is like a sponge that absorbs all the water to gain the most insight from another's perspective.

This is the relationship between a teacher and a student, a guru and a disciple. This learning and enlightenment experience occurs all the time, every day, through conversation and reflection. We are all students to some and teachers to some and to some we are a bit of both. Even within your Self there is both a teacher and a student.

This part of the book is a result of what happened today after talking with a dear friend, my improv-acting teacher. It was inspired by what he taught me about listening. It resonates with what another dear friend taught me about silence and truth.

Listening to the silence within your Self to align with truth is the key. This is how we can align with the Divine. Surrender to Gods Will. Live in Harmony with Nature.

What Leads?

God, nature, being, inner vision, speech, and the willingness to go into the unknown.

Whose desires are you feeling? Are they yours? Who are you? What part of you is desiring? Where are your desires coming from? Social conditioning? Ego gains? Nature? God?

If it is Nature's desire, Nature will manifest it. Not even an Emperor can defeat a desireless man. You don't have to try to become desireless. That process will happen naturally with experience and knowledge.

As human beings, we have the potential to evolve and become an instrument of Nature, a conduit for God, a tool for the Divine. This doesn't necessarily mean we will all be able to walk on water and fly. Not until we hit the tipping point anyway, when it isn't such a far-out belief in what is possible. Sat Yuga? But it starts with listening. The process of tuning your instrument (the human body/mind/soul) can be done and is being done whether we are aware of it or not. And, the more aware or conscious we become, the faster we can evolve.

It is all a matter of consciousness. The simplest form of awareness. That is all we need to lead us. Conscious awareness. Listen. Meditate.

Practice what you want to become. Surrender to Nature.

You don't have to worry about having or suppressing desires. Accept what arises within you and allow your awareness to organize what you need. You don't have to force your will to make things happen. If *It* is Nature's desire, *It* will manifest, and you will know what action needs to be taken spontaneously when the time comes.

Patience is a virtue.

Thoughts from Being AKA "Contemplations"

What thoughts have not been thought? Are there patterns in the thoughts we have? Are those patterns of thought founded on what our core beliefs are? Do we choose our core beliefs, or do they develop over time through experience and socialization? Is there something deeper than belief?

From my experience, it appears that my thoughts arise in my mind where feelings arise in my heart/chest area. If there is something deeper than belief, how is that experienced? Could it be that the experience of the mind and body functioning together as one is a unification of thought and feeling? Unification of our hearts and minds? What do we call this? Being? Consciousness?

Does our state of being or consciousness underlie all of our thoughts and feelings? If this state of being or consciousness is there? How can we access it? Meditation? Contemplation? Yoga? Can complete devotion or attention to any activity unify the mind and body? Unification of our hearts and minds?

Can this be considered the power of awareness? Concentrated power of will? What is the benefit of having one pointed focus or this power of awareness that opens the doors to access the full range of possible thoughts and feelings?

Understanding? Understanding the experience of having thoughts and feelings? They come and go, do they not? Some are repeated more than others, do they not? Can we change our patterns of thought and feeling? How?

By identifying with the power of awareness? Meditation? Contemplation? Yoga? Complete devotion or attention to any activity to unify the mind and body? Unification of our hearts and minds?

This section is titled thoughts from being, which is another way of saying contemplation. This is the type of thinking that allows you to search within your own being to discover your true Nature. This type of thought experiment requires an inward dive into the unknown—the mind being open to itself for examination.

Free from Resistance

Do we choose our thoughts or do our thoughts choose us? Is it the seeking of truth that delivers us to it or it to us? Is that the power of intention?

With my attention turned inward, the questions arise along with their answers. But sometimes, the answers are only as clear as the questions. The interplay of thoughts between who I think I am with what comes through my mind and body. Who or what is it that thinks my thoughts and feels my feelings?

My thoughts … my feelings.

I am the "experiencer" of thoughts and emotions. Free from resistance, I understand. Free from resistance and judgment in this moment, I accept what is. Thoughts come and go. Feelings come and go. People come and go. I recognize the extent of my own ignorance and surrender to what is. In the silence, I feel most present. Behind these eyes, I dwell.

What have "I" lost? What have "I" gained? Depending on who "I" identify with the answer differs. If "I" identify with, Dustin Matthews, my ego, my persona, "I" have lost and gained a lot. If "I" identify with my higher Self or my soul or the universal consciousness within me. It's all the same. But "I" feel as though "I" oscillate between identifying with myself as Dustin and my Self as God. Dustin within God. God within Dustin.

We are all that way. We are all connected to the divine and can experience divinity within ourselves. But when our small self or ego is in pain it's important to remember the higher Self or the God within each of us. That is where we pull our strength and equanimity from.

The pendulum swings; throughout the days, the weeks, the months, the years.

Left, right, left, right, left right.

Love, pain, love, pain, love, pain.

Loss, gain, loss, gain, loss, gain.

-DUSTIN MATTHEWS (TO BE DETERMINED)

This is the rhythm of life. The cycle of existence. Resisting the inevitability of love and pain only adds to the suffering.

Life and destiny are like quicksand.

The harder you fight it, the faster you drown.

The faster you drown, the scarier it becomes.

The scarier it becomes, the harder you fight it.

Stop resisting and rise to become.

-DUSTIN MATTHEWS (TO BE DETERMINED)

The cycle repeats until you learn the lesson. Fighting it is resisting it. Accept it. And be free. Whatever it is for you, it is, for you.

Accept it. And be free. The intellectual understanding can only provide a piece of the puzzle. Experiencing it for yourself is where the true liberation comes into play.

How?

Wake. Breathe. Meditate. Eat. Sleep. Repeat.

The patterns of life unfold throughout life.

Observe. Adapt. Observe. Adapt. Observe. Adapt.

Easy to say. Harder to do.

This doesn't mean you won't be free from experiencing thoughts and emotions. The way out is through. If you kink a hose and try to stop the water from flowing, pressure will build up in the hose. The water is still in there. It will come out eventually or the hose will break. The water in this analogy represents what it is we resist.

In this analogy, we are like the hose. Let It flow through you and It will pass. Be like water, free of resistance.

Reality and Liberation

Is everything we do just our attempt to pacify ourselves from facing the realities of existence? Do we try to stay busy, busy, busy, so that the deeper existential thoughts don't scare us into facing reality? Realization. Reality. What is real?

Facing reality can sometimes cause a lot of grief and sadness. The stages of grief are denial, anger, bargaining, depression, and acceptance. When you start facing reality, you can start experiencing these things. You can get a dose of reality and then try to avoid it, thinking that distractions will numb the pain.

I think everyone wants to accept reality and some probably think they do accept reality. But it takes a strong will to self-reflect and be honest about what you see. It's not always easy. But it always comes back to being. The simple act of being.

Contemplation of these existential questions to some can seem scary and hard to face but with more depth comes more discovery and with more discovery comes more acceptance of what is. More peace. More calm. More stability.

- Believe it or not, it takes great strength to sit and be still.

- To witness your thoughts come and go without letting them become you. To witness your thoughts come and go. *Unattached.*

- To witness your feelings come and go without letting them become you. To witness your feelings come and go. *Unattached.*

- To witness your behaviors come and go without letting them become you. To witness your behaviors come and go. *Unattached.*

To merely exist and watch thoughts come and go without needing to go get a coffee, go smoke a cigarette, go to work, go work out, go watch a movie, go shopping, go hang out with friends, go for a run. Go, go, go—do, do, do. Are these activities you want to enjoy? Are they part of your routine? Or are these just habitual behaviors that keep you from facing a deeper reality?

Do we fear the depth and reality of existence, so we stay on the surface to protect ourselves? And when faced with the existential questions or deeper realities, are they too difficult to cope with, so we feel pain and suffering and reach for things to pacify and keep us busy? Is it the fear of death that scares us? Or is it the fear of the unknown?

What happens when we die?

Isn't that the question we all want an answer to?

Does it all just end?

Do we dissolve back into Unity with the vast emptiness of All That Is?

Do we have a meeting with God?

Does our soul/consciousness reincarnate?

If we are able to accept the unknown and face it free from fear, don't we feel free?

Is this liberation?

Surrender to being?

So now that you understand that we might not understand how it works …

What do you want to do?

You want to go get a coffee?

You want to write some more?

You want to go deeper?

If this has made sense to you so far, you probably want to go deeper.

If it isn't making sense to you yet. Reread it. Meditate. Contemplate it.

Let it go. Come back to it. Come back to being.

It's simpler than you might think.

You get it now?

Come back to being.

Thoughts come up and we experience feelings as we observe this inner and outer world.

Come back to being.

I have bills to pay, I'm hungry, I don't like my job.

Come back to being.

Silence.

Thoughts. Thoughts. Thoughts.

Mantra. Mantra. Mantra.

Silence.

Peace.

Bliss.

Thank You to My Transcendental Meditation Teachers

Transcendental Meditation is a life-changing practice, which is very simple to learn. Anyone can do it. It is very easy and natural. You just have to learn the practice and in time you will see. Transcendental Meditation is what helps me in a way words cannot explain. I thank my teachers Bill and Joan for sharing this practice with me as well as Maharishi Mahesh Yogi for his wisdom. Jai Guru Dev.

I also want to thank all of my professors and colleagues from Maharishi International University who led me further to gain more of an in-depth understanding of this knowledge. Thank you to my parents and my sister. Thank you to all of my family and friends. Thank you, God. Thank you, Self. Jai Guru Dev.

Ideas for Global Solutions

- **Education**—Education is what will save the world. Citizens of the world should be allowed a free education and the only factor that should determine their acceptance into educational programs should be the individual's ability to meet the educational standards. Meditation should be available, optional and free to learn in all schools.

- **Climate change**—The climate is changing with or without us. If we want to prolong our existence, we need to live in harmony with the planet that provides us with what we need to survive: clean air, water, food. Stop what we're doing that causes damage to the climate and adjust our ways to slow the dangerous changes that are increasing our risk of extinction. Reduce or eliminate carbon emissions, use of fossil fuels, mass production of animal farms, and mass agriculture. Find sustainable solutions.

- **Overpopulation**—Education. Abstinence. Simplicity or Minimalism. Reducing the materialistic over consumption of products and goods. Maybe space travel but best to make Earth a safe home again.

- **Exhausting natural resources**—What are our needs? Do we have enough? What should we change? Do we consume too much? What do we really need?

- **Renewable resources**—What resources are renewable? How can we utilize them? Reuse recycled materials. What forms of sustainable energy can we use? What is preventing us from using these forms of sustainable energy? Technology? Money? Political/ Economic Control?

- **The facts**—What are the facts? Truth in education is essential.

- **The story**—The stories we're told can be propaganda to get us to believe certain things and act in conditioned ways. What are the stories we're being told? What is the truth?

- **Money**—The love of money is the root of all evil.

All wrongdoing can be traced to an excessive attachment to material wealth.

-APOSTLE PAUL

- **Healthcare and housing**—Free universal healthcare and housing for those who need it.

- **Business solutions**—Big businesses should help play a larger role in global solutions.

Solutions Based on Maslow's Hierarchy of Needs

All human physiological needs met first. Safety. Oxygen. Water. Food. Sleep.

Security needs second. Home. Financial stability.

Love and connection.

Esteem.

Self-actualization.

My Personal Stuff

What follows are a few sample poems, sayings, daily checklists, and images that have inspired me along my journey. I hope you enjoyed this guide and will use it whenever you need a little pick me up or realignment on your path.

Creating this book was a wonderful experience because I was living through each of these steps as I wrote them. It was a transformative process that opened my mind to a whole new world. I would like to thank God and the Universe for all of this. I've never been a man of a strict religion, but I do believe in a higher power. I do believe the practice of Transcendental Meditation has had tremendous benefits. I do believe all religions are like rivers stemming from the same source.

Thank you, Mom, Dad, and Emilia, for all of your love and support. I know it was hard at times, but I'm grateful to have you as my family. Without my mother and father's love and support, I would not be alive. I love you both more than you know. Momma, I love you. Dad, you're my Hero. Thank you for your patience, love, and support. Thank you to all of my aunts, uncles, grandparents, and cousins. Thank you to my Uncle Scotty for helping me out in a time of need and providing me with the opportunity to work with you and learn from you.

A huge thank you to the teachers and coaches that I've had throughout my life. Thank you for your love, patience, and lessons. I'm grateful to have learned from you. Thank you to all of my friends, teammates, classmates, and roommates. I hope you're doing well; I love you all! A special thank you to my football coach Paul Castonia for all you've taught me over the years. It continues to serve me well.

Thank you all so much for your friendship, love and continued support.

My Daily Checklist

- Make my bed

- Gratitude prayers

- Look in the mirror and say, *I love you.*

- Meditate

- Work out

- Eat healthy

- Master my crafts: writing, rapping, and acting

- Work toward achieving my goals

- Say, *Thank you and I love you,* to Mom and Dad.

- Have faith in life. Love for today. And hope for tomorrow.

Daily Reminders

Following a daily checklist will allow you to stick to a routine and stay on course.

Developing this daily checklist is different for everybody.

Some examples for your daily checklist follow.

- **Make the bed**—Complete this task each morning before anything else. This is the first opportunity of the day to complete a task successfully. It is a stepping-stone and a confidence booster for the day ahead. Completing a task successfully is contagious and will provide you with the will to complete more tasks successfully. And even if you don't complete anymore tasks successfully on that given day. You will have hope for tomorrow with your nicely made bed.

- **Gratitude**—You should be grateful for everything you do have. You should say thank you for everything you have in your life. You choose what you are grateful for. Practice it daily. Every morning after making the bed and every night before going to sleep, try saying the *Gratitude Prayers*. Thank you, God, for my life, love, hope, faith, knowledge and understanding. Thank you, God, for my family, friends, teachers, coaches, teammates, bosses, coworkers, clients, and all other people in this life. Thank you, God, for my health, wealth, and happiness. Thank you, God, for my big, strong healthy mind, body, and spirit. Thank you, God, for my strength, drive, and determination. Thank you, God, for my positive attitude. I love you. Thank you … The list can go on, but these are some key things to be grateful for. Sometimes, I'll imagine if I woke up and no longer had the things, I didn't say thank you for the night before. It really gets me going. The list just keeps on growing. Gratitude has a kind of gravitational effect because it attracts more of what we are grateful for.

- **Vision board**—Create a vision board with motivational quotes, pictures of things you love and want to manifest into this world, and a list of your goals. Take time each day to look at this vision board and stay on course or adjust accordingly. Read your goals daily. Develop a plan of action to reach them and continue to learn, act, and adjust to make these goals come true. Sometimes, drawing these goals as pictures or creating them on the computer is a helpful way to make them more personal and unique.

- *The Man in the Glass* by **Peter Dale Wimbrow Sr.** Read this poem and look into the eyes of the man in the glass every day. Can you look your Self in the eye and say, "I love you?"

- **Write**—Writing is a great way to deal with and express your emotions. It allows you a way in which you can play out different situations and ponder the decisions, actions, and consequences that follow. When you let yourself go and just write it, it's freeing, and it soothes the soul.

- **Sayings/prayers**—Try to find a saying that you can tell yourself when you're down or feeling negative. Something to bring you back to the present, out of the past, and hopeful about the future. Finding what works may take some practice and time. It is different for everybody and for different situations and circumstances. Finding something positive and spiritually uplifting is best. Below are a few examples that I use depending on the situation and circumstances.

1. When negative thoughts are taking over.

   Try saying: *Let it come. Let it go. Breathe. Let it come. Let it go. Breathe.*

2. When facing difficulty with addiction/discipline/sacrifice.

   Try saying: *Thank you, God, for my strength.* Or: *Thank you, God, for my sobriety.*

3. When in need of releasing negative emotions.

Try saying: *Thank you, God, for freeing me from these negative thoughts and emotions.*

4. When dealing with lost love/death/regret.

   Try saying: *Thank you, God, for my life. Thank you, God, for providing me with the opportunity to live a life in surrender and of service to you.*

- **Transcendental Meditation**—Meditation is like educated medication. The benefits of meditation are life changing. Anyone can do it. You just have to learn how. Try it for your Self. You'll get It—eventually.

- **Eating healthy and exercise**—It is a lifestyle. A healthier, happier life starts with a healthy diet and exercise routine. Try eating more fresh/raw/local/organic fruits and vegetables. Nuts, beans, and seeds are a great source of protein for vegetarians.

- **Live in the present**—You cannot change the past. You can only learn from it. Control what you can control. Focus on what you are doing in the present. Live Right Now. Think positive. Be grateful. Love and learn.

Today is the only day. Now is the only time.

-DUSTIN MATTHEWS (TO BE DETERMINED)

I believe it's the desire for self-knowledge or how to make one's self better that will promote our individual well-being and the well-being of the collective. Our own personal growth will have a ripple effect throughout society.

DUSTIN MATTHEWS (TO BE DETERMINED)

Thank you for reading *IMAGINE: The Simple Steps To Success.* If you'd like to access more of the content I'm developing please visit my web page. www.dustinmatthewsmedia.com

Thank you! Good luck! God Bless!

REFERENCE LIST

Bogoda, R. (1996). *A Simple Guide to Life*. Access to Insight (BCBS Edition). Retrieved from https://www.accesstoinsight.org/lib/authors/bogoda/wheel397.html

Csikszentmihalyi, Mihaly. (1990). *Flow: The Psychology of Optimal Experience*. Harper & Row: New York, NY.

Hagelin, J. (December 4, 2019). A Scientific Perspective by Quantum Physicist John Hagelin, PhD. Retrieved from https://tmhome.com/uncategorized/scientific-perspective-quantum-physicist-john-hagelin-phd/

Hagelin, J. (October 25, 2016). Consciousness is the Unified Field – Quantum Physicist John Hagelin, PhD. Retrieved from https://transcendentalmeditationblog.wordpress.com/2016/10/25/consciousness-is-the-unified-field-quantum-physicist-john-hagelin/

Hardy, D. (2010). *The Compound Effect*. Da Capo Press: Philadelphia, PA.

Keane, B. (2017). *The Fitness Mindset*. Rethink Press Limited: Gorleston-on-Sea, United Kingdom.

Mahesh Yogi, M. (1963). *Science of Being and Art of Living*. Maharishi Vedic University Press: Vlodrop, The Netherlands.

Mahesh Yogi, M. (1967). *Maharishi Mahesh Yogi on the Bhagavad Gita.* Penguin Group: London, England.

Maslow, A. (1943). *A Theory of Human Motivation.* Martino Fine Books: Eastford, CT.

Scott, S.J. (2014) *SMART Goals Made Simple.* Archangel Ink.

Three Initiates. (1908) *Kybalion.* Yogi Publication Society: Chicago, IL. Retrieved from https://www.google.com/books/edition/The_Kybalion/T3FRAAAAYAAJ?hl=en&gbpv=1&printsec=frontcover

Travis, F. (2012). *Your Brain is a River, Not a Rock.* CreateSpace Independent Publishing Platform: Scotts Valley, CA.

Walker, M. (2017). *Why We Sleep: Unlocking the Power of Sleep and Dreams.* Penguin Random House: New York City, NY.